BEST "NEW" AFRICAN POETS 2023 ANTHOLOGY/ ANTHOLOGIE DES MEILLEURS "NOUVEAUX" POÈTES AFRICAINS 2023/ ANTOLOGIA DOS MELHORES "NOVOS" AFRICANOS 2023

Edited and Compiled by:
Tendai Rinos Mwanaka
Helder Simbad
Gerald Mpesse

Mwanaka Media and Publishing Pvt Ltd,
Chitungwiza Zimbabwe
*
Creativity, Wisdom and Beauty

Publisher: *Mmap*
Mwanaka Media and Publishing Pvt Ltd
24 Svosve Road, Zengeza 1
Chitungwiza Zimbabwe
mwanaka@yahoo.com
mwanaka13@gmail.com
https://www.mmapublishing.org
www.africanbookscollective.com/publishers/mwanaka-media-and-publishing
https://facebook.com/MwanakaMediaAndPublishing/

Distributed in and outside N. America by African Books Collective
orders@africanbookscollective.com
www.africanbookscollective.com

ISBN: 978-1-77933-171-7
EAN: 9781779331717

© Tendai Rinos Mwanaka 2023

All rights reserved.
No part of this book may be reproduced or transmitted in any form or by any means, mechanical or electronic, including photocopying and recording, or be stored in any information storage or retrieval system, without written permission from the publisher

DISCLAIMER
All views expressed in this publication are those of the author and do not necessarily reflect the views of *Mmap*.

TABLE OF CONTENTS

POETRY: *Aminu Femi Jamiu (Nigeria)*
SOUL: *Aminu Femi Jamiu*
WE ARE HUMANS TOO: *Aminu Femi Jamiu*
INE NDEPAPA: *Austin Kaluba (Zambia)*
IT SURPRISES ME (English translation): *Austin Kaluba*
ABASUNGU BANEMBO: *Austin Kaluba*
WHITES WITH INCISIONS (English translation): *Austin Kaluba*
INSEKU: *Austin Kaluba*
WEEDS (English translation): *Austin Kaluba*
Dear Golden Eyed Lady: *Abbas Muhammad Usman (Nigeria)*
Missive To Saharan Princess: *Abbas Muhammad Usman*
The Secret: *Abbas Muhammad Usman*
Four by Four: *Lucas Zulu (South Africa)*
The sightseer: *Lucas Zulu*
Beyond the War: *Oladele Babajamu (Nigeria)*
THIS IS OUR TIME: *Oladele Babajamu*
THE BOAT OF LIFE: *Oladele Babajamu*
THE PREDATOR STILL ROAMS AROUND: *Geraldo Bleza Malota (Malawi)*
THAT LUCK CHARM: *Geraldo Bleza Malota*
AFRICA DON'T BLINK: *Geraldo Bleza Malota*
Made in the oven: *Justice Masangano (Malawi)*
I call it my freedom: *Justice Masangano*
The future: *Justice Masangano*
Dream of Desperation: *Alshaad Kara (Mauritius)*
Spirit of the Heart: *Alshaad Kara*
Men of Africa: *Alshaad Kara*
THIS NIGHT IS A HALLOWEEN NIGHT: *Emmanuel Douglas Mulomole (Malawi)*
THE RECONCILIATORY VOICE: *Emmanuel Douglas Mulomole*
THE STRENGTH OF HOPE: *Emmanuel Douglas Mulomole*
EPICEDIUM: *Emmanuel Tumwesige (Uganda)*
THE DIFFERENT SIMILARITY: *Emmanuel Tumwesige*

I MISS YOU: *Emmanuel Tumwesige*
THE WIND BRINGS SONGS: *Emman Usman Shehu (Nigeria)*
WHY DO THEY SAY THE DAY BREAKS?: *Emman Usman Shehu*
SEASON'S EXTRACT: *Emman Usman Shehu*
war reads like a poem: *Keketso Adorn Mashigo (South Africa)*
when home is the only place: *Keketso Adorn Mashigo*
the silence that nip the good bud: *Keketso Adorn Mashigo*
to catch an oyster: *Archie Swanson (South Africa)*
sangoma: *Archie Swanson*
finding Sugar Man: *Archie Swanson*
WALL: *Abdullatif Khalid (Uganda)*
PSYCHE IS NATURAL: *Abdullatif Khalid*
THE TRUE REASON: *Abdullatif Khalid*
THE OTHER SIDE OF TOWN: *Ojonugwa John Attah (Nigeria)*
I HAVE LOST MY FREEDOM: *Ojonugwa John Attah*
WHEN HOME CALLS, YOU SHOULD ANSWER: *Ojonugwa John Attah*
My Father: *William Khalipwina Mpina (Malawi)*
I Still Remember: *William Khalipwina Mpina*
My Mother Suffered: *William Khalipwina Mpina*
Gurkha: *Goodenough Mashego (South Africa)*
39 & 41: *Goodenough Mashego*
erasure: *Goodenough Mashego*
Adventure: *Martin Chrispine Juwa (Malawi)*
Life in the smartphone age: *Martin Chrispine Juwa*
Wishes: *Martin Chrispine Juwa*
BABA VAENDA: *Andrey B. Matambo (Zambia)*
DESPERATION: *Andrey B. Matambo*
THE A.I COUP: *Andrey B. Matambo*
Sex and Poetry: *Edward Dzonze (Zimbabwe)*
Waiting for the Rain: *Edward Dzonze*
Wet dreams from the heavens: *Edward Dzonze*
IHEANYICHI: *Chisimdi George (Nigeria)*
COUPLING: *Adiela Akoo (South Africa)*
as the rain pitter-pattered: *Adiela Akoo*
MILITOCRACY: *Dickson Saba (Nigeria)*

WHAT A COLD WORLD: *Dickson Saba*
CELESTIAL REFLECTION: *Dickson Saba*
what 'll they be seeing?: *Chenjerai Mhondera (Zimbabwe)*
calling: *Chenjerai Mhondera*
IT WILL BE OKAY: *Antreka Tladi (South Africa)*
A BRIGHT FACE, A GUIDING LIGHT: *Antreka Tladi*
The Stench: *Jabulani Mzinyathi (Zimbabwe)*
On The Prowl: *Jabulani Mzinyathi*
The Same Dog: *Jabulani Mzinyathi*
A Hooligan's Dark Paradise: *Joseph Daniel Sukali (Malawi)*
Aborted at Birth: *Joseph Daniel Sukali*
Where Do We Go When We Sleep: *Joseph Daniel Sukali*
Burnt Offerings: *Kennix Odera (Kenya)*
After life: *Kennix Odera*
HIS Majesty the QUEEN: *Kennix Odera*
Wakeful: *Philip Miti (Zambia)*
She Melting Me To Love: *Philip Miti*
You're A True Friend Of Yourself: *Philip Miti*
The universe: *Abigirl Phiri (Zimbabwe)*
Ode to a pen: *Abigirl Phiri*
Zim now: *Abigirl Phiri*
Beautiful: *Adaobi Charlyn Chilekezi (Nigeria)*
I am a winner!: *Adaobi Charlyn Chilekezi*
Altered spirits: *Adaobi Charlyn Chilekezi*
Like the starry night sky: *Obinna Chilekezi (Nigeria)*
A change of taste: *Obinna Chilekezi*
Good: *Obinna Chilekezi*
Darling star!: *Adebayo julius O (Nigeria)*
Time flies!: *Adebayo julius O*
A PLACE CALLED HOME: *Adebayo julius O*
PYRAYERS END HERE: *Lucas Lungu Jr | HOLY POET (Zambia)*
GOD BLESS YOUR SINS: *Lucas Lungu Jr | HOLY POET*
MY COUNTRY: *Salmista Cortês (Angola)*
I WISH IF I HAD WINGS: *Salmista Cortês*
THE BLACK CRY TO MOTHER AFRICA: *Salmista Cortês*
Stops in a Winged Bracket: *Okolo Chinua (Nigeria)*
Hands Sardined in Gold: *Okolo Chinua*

On The Journey of Returning: *Okolo Chinua*
The End of the Road: *McLayode (Nigeria)*
The Songs for and of a Benedict: *McLayode*
Tyrant Time: *McLayode*
The Marvel of the Dandelion: *Colleen Venter (South Africa)*
I live in Fear: *David Chasumba (Zimbabwe)*
On Turning Fifty: *David Chasumba*
The Daddy Issues: *David Chasumba*
WEAVER BIRDS: *Alfred S. Mukanaka (Zambia)*
THE MAGICIAN IN MY BED: *Womba Nakazwe (Zambia)*
You Have Come Again: *Wellington Nwogu (Nigeria)*
BAD DEBTS: *Kimutai Kemboi Allan (Kenya)*
MASQUES OF DECEIT: *Kimutai Kemboi Allan*
TO DISCOMBOBULATE: *Kimutai Kemboi Allan*
HOW MY BROTHER PRONOUNCES HOME: *Tajudeen Muadh (Nigeria)*
MY HOME, IS NOT A CADAVER OF ROSES: *Tajudeen Muadh*
BREAKING: *Tajudeen Muadh*
Pieces of Mirrored Light: *Isaac Kilibwa (Kenya)*
Sandra: *Isaac Kilibwa*
Hope Awake: *Isaac Kilibwa*
Requiem: Lekki Tollgate: *Prosper Ifeanyi (Nigeria)*
Summarised Women: *Prosper Ifeanyi*
a poem// in which freedom means my father & his inadequacies: *Prosper Ifeanyi*
I WHINED MY WAIST ROUND THE WORLD, A WHILE AGO: *Onatola Abiodun (Nigeria)*
SILTING 6: *Onatola Abiodun*
/!!!\: *Onatola Abiodun*
in this city: *MK Kuol (South Sudan)*
times like this: *MK Kuol*
epitaphs: *MK Kuol*
Bulawayo: *Tembi Charles (Zimbabwe)*
ELES SABEM!?: *Afonso Kudissadila (Angola)*
MARCAS DO SÉCULO XX: *Afonso Kudissadila*
RAZÕES PARA VIVER & PARA MORRER: *Armando Botelho (Angola)*

SENTI MENTALISTA(S) GLORIOSO(S): *Armando Botelho*
HOMEN: *Destino Ventura (Angola)*
FONTE: *Destino Ventura*
nas pegadas do pássaro: *Dnaffe Medina (Agola)*
dimoyo: *Dnaffe Medina*
Magras silhuetas: *Hélder Simbad (Angola)*
Meu Coração é sua Praça: *Hélder Simbad*
Bolo em Fatias: *Hélder Simbad*
Delírios no pulmão da noite (Alias ou aluas?): *Henriques Fortuna (Angola)*
Lunática comiseração: *Henriques Fortuna*
Rugas no Sol: *Isabel Sango (Angola)*
Uigense: *Isabel Sango*
Intensa Paixão: *Isabel Sango*
A cada minuto: *João Horácio Alexandrino (Angola)*
Sou uma criança perdida: *João Horácio Alexandrino*
Muro que há por detrás do mundo: *João Horácio Alexandrino*
guardiã da vida: *Khilson Khalunga (Angola)*
plano eleito oral: *Khilson Khalunga*
ESQUIZOFRÊNICO TEMPO II: *Luís Kapemba (Angola)*
DUAS PALMAS DE PURGATÓRIO: *Luís Kapemba*
BICHINHOS NA PRAIA: *Maria Manuel Menezes (Angola, Sao Tome and Principe)*
ZUNGUEIRAS "NO" MUSSULO: *Maria Manuel Menezes*
NÃO AO RACISMO: *Maria Manuel Menezes*
VAZIO: *Mwene XI (Angola)*
ÁFRICA ERRANTE: *Mwene XI*
MENTE: *Mwene XI*
NÃO JAMAIS: *Ntony Kunsevi (Angola)*
MISTÉRIO: *Ntony Kunsevi*
QUARENTONA: *Ntony Kunsevi*
AR TE FILOSOFANDO: *Satchonga Tchiwale (Angola)*
RUPTURA AOS PATRIOTAS: *Satchonga Tchiwale*
RUPTURA AOS GOVERNANTES: *Satchonga Tchiwale*
LABIRINTO: *Simão Nzombo Antônio (Angola)*
SERENATA ANORGÁSMICA: *Simão Nzombo Antônio*
Lweji: *Vítor Ricardo (Angola)*

Mulemba solitária: *Vítor Ricardo*
Grotte secrète : *Laroche Ngodjo Abata (Cameroun)*
Élèves... : *Laroche Ngodjo Abata*
Souvenir : *Laroche Ngodjo Abata*
Village des fous : *Arnold Mondo K (République Démocratique du Congo)*
A la belle aux cieux : *Arnold Mondo K*
Cantique africain : *Arnold Mondo K*
Bronzitude : *Michel Dongmo Evina (Cameroun)*
Le feu du milieu : *Michel Dongmo Evina*
Réminiscences : *Faustin Junior Embolo Embolo (Cameroun)*
L'Afrique contaminée : *Corneille Mbonyi (République démocratique du Congo)*
A toi Afrique : *Serge Billo Ebanga (Cameroun)*
J'ai rêvé de toi Afrique : *Serge Billo Ebanga*
Oublier : *Chandra Feupessi*
Best New African Poets Collaboration : *Curated by Tendai Rinos Mwanaka*
Best New African Poets Interview: *Tendai Rinos Mwanaka*

About editors

Tendai Rinos Mwanaka is a multidisciplinary artist, editor, publisher and producer with 26 individual books and over 27 curated anthologies published in US, Northern Ireland, UK, Cameroon and Zimbabwe. He has 3 music albums playing in at least 18 radio stations in US, Canada, UK, France, Israel, Brazil and Australia and hundreds of paintings and drawings, thousands of photographs, some exhibited, published and sold. His art pieces and writing has appeared in over 400 journals in over 35 countries and translated into at least 11 languages. His music can be licensed here https://www.songtradr.com/tendai.mwanaka Find him here: https://m.facebook.com/tendai.mwanaka

Hélder Simbad é poeta. Em muitos casos, é professor não assalariado; quando quer irritar os outros, gosta de brincar de crítico literário. Não é um gajo muito sério, mas venceu o prémio literário António Jacinto 2017 com a obra Enviesada Rosa. Como o presente livro é de poesia apenas, publicou também o livro Insurreição dos Signos e mais nada. O resto é zunga.

Géraldin MPESSE vit et écrit à Yaoundé. Il est auteur d'un recueil de poèmes en langue espagnole. En 2018, il publie, avec les écrivains argentins, une anthologie : *Palabras tabuadas*. Le jeune écrivain a publié des poèmes dans la revue (en ligne) *Le capital de mots*. Il écrit également pour *Clijec Mag'*. Par ailleurs, il a été le président du comité d'organisation de la 3ᵉ édition du FESTAE (Festival africain des écrivains émergents). Enseignant d'espagnol et étudiant-chercheur en Langues Africaines et Linguistique à l'Université de Yaoundé I ; actuellement, il est le directeur de publication de *Lepan Africa Revista*.

Contributors' Bio Notes

Aminu Femi Jamiu is an Internationally recognized, Award-Winning Nigerian Poet, Author, Editor, Social Activist, International Ambassador Of Peace, Universal Icon Of Poetry, recipient of several National and International Awards, including the Gujarat Sahitya academy award. He was born on 26th October 1994. He is an HND holder of Biochemistry from Kogi State Polytechnic, lokoja, Nigeria. Femi has authored two English poetry book "Poetry Pearls" and "Cosmic Voice" (The International Anthology of Contemporary Global Poets), co-author of 15 Anthologies. His poems have been published in many Magazines, Journals, E-zines and Newspapers. His poems have been translated into many International languages. Recently his poem has been published in Guinness World Record holding Anthology. He has been featured as one of the World's Contemporary poet. He's the founder and president of the international literary online platform "Home of Global Writers.

Austin Kaluba was born in Northern Zambia and studied journalism at Africa Literature Centre in Kitwe. He was editor of the Sunday Times of Zambia before being appointed as a diplomat to the United Kingdom. He studied Creative Writing from the Oxford University (Department for continuing education). His collection of short stories *Mensah's London Blues and other Stories* has been published in the UK by Carnelian Heart Publishing. He has translated several works into ci-Bemba among them *The Pilgrim's Progress, Animal Farm and Le Petit Prince*. His poetry has appeared in literary journals and anthologies in Europe, Asia and Africa.

Abbas Muhammad Usman, is Nigerian poet, writer and youth activist, living in Gombe State Nigeria. His a published writer by many magazines within and outside Nigeria. He is currently pursuing his first degree in the field of pharmacy at University of Maiduguri Borno state.

Lucas Zulu is an award-winning poet, writer, publisher and anthologist. His works has appeared in Canada, Zimbabwe, Cameroon, Singapore, Ireland, Nigeria, India, Malaysia, Botswana and United States of America, a resident of Emalahleni, Kwa-Quqa, Mpumalanga Province. He writes both in English and Zulu and studied Transportation Management at University of Johannesburg.

Oladele Babajamu is a fellow of the National Defence College of Nigeria who retired in the rank of Colonel from the Nigerian Army in 2011. He was PRO (N) of the Association of Nigerian Authors and also a two-term Chairman of the Kwara State chapter of the Association. His oeuvre includes *The Security Banquet 2022, From Grass to Greatness* 2020 amongst others. His poems have appeared in various anthologies *LIWURAMS 2021, ANA Review2021, Timeless Treasures 2017, Timeless Voices 2006 and Five Hundred Nigerian Poets 2005* amongst others.

Geraldo Bleza Malota is a Malawian Poet and writer. He is a young Catholic Priest from the Diocese of Dedza. He was born on 27th June 1998. He is a holder of a Bachelor's Degree in Philosophy and a Bachelor's Degree in Theology both obtained from the Catholic University of Malawi. Malota has written and contributed numerous articles and poetic pieces in many magazines. He is the author of literature anthology titled *Tales of a Sojourner*. He is also one of the founding members and Editor of The Sprout Magazine. He is still working on various upcoming projects.

Justice Masangano: I am a creative writer from Malawi. I have published my pieces with our local newspaper and magazines as well as a number of online poetry groups since 2004. Notable international publications include *GRAINS: a journal, BARD'S DAY KEGS: Inspirational quotes, BRAVE VOICES and praxis magazine*.

Alshaad Kara is a Mauritian poet who writes from his heart. He won the 2023 "Zheng Nian Cup" Literary Award Third Prize. His latest poems were published in "The BeZine", "Men Matters Online Journal" and "Slamming Bricks Anthology 3rd Edition".

Emmanuel Douglas Mulomole was born on 8th December. He is from southern Africa, Blantyre Malawi. He is a poet, Freelance writer, Quote developer, Peace activist and short story writer. He is a bronze categorized member of the largest platform literary group Motivational Strips. He has received many certificates from the various International forums. His writings have greatly been published on frabjous blogs or websites that verisimilarly promotes literature. Some poems which is dexterously written by Emmanuel, have been featured in some volumes of *Brave Voice Poetry Journal (Zimbabwe)*. And his poems have also been featured in international anthologies by poetry namely...

My name is Emmanuel Tumwesige, a poet from Uganda. I am an educator at secondary level of English language and literature in English, plus General knowledge. My writing started with prose and later got inspiration of poetry from songs; passion growing after joining the school and church choirs. Most of my writings are based on events unfolding around me and stories I hear from people about what they experience. Sometimes I don't intend to write about them but I find myself drafting something which later develops into a topic and I finally map it up.

Emman Usman Shehu hails from Maradun, Zamfara State of Nigeria. He currently resides in Abuja, Nigeria's capital, where he works with the Internatonal Institute of Journalism. He is also involved with the Abuja Writers Forum (AWF), and is the editor of the literary journals - Cavalcade and Dugwe. Passionate about facilitating writing workshops, his poems have appeared in several print and online publications, including *Okike, Kakaki ,Sentinel Poetry, PoetryWales, Stone Throw, Panoply and Best New African Poets Anthology.* He has published four poetry collectons: *Questions For Big Brother, Open Sesame, Icarus Rising and The River Never Returns*

Keketso Adorn Mashigo is the author of a short stories collection entitled *Sofina is Not the End*. He is a poet and co-author of an essays anthology entitled *Shadows of Their Mothers*. Mashigo is also a book reviewer at Pulp Review, a proof-reader, pro-Palestine and freelance journalist. His work has been featured on many different publications including the *Loocha Magazine, The New Coin, Pangolin Review, the Kalahari Review, Praxis Online, AfricanWriter and Avbob Poetry*. Mashigo writes in Madjembeni, the rural Bushbuckridge in Mpumalanaga, South Africa.

Archie Swanson's poems have been published in *Stanzas* and *New Contrast* magazines, the *Best New African Poetry* anthologies, and Spanish National Newspaper *El Mundo*, and have been shortlisted for the European Union Sol Plaatje Award and UK Bridport Prize. In 2019, 'my Guernica' placed second in the English section of the AVBOB Poetry Competition. Set to music, poems have been performed in London's Wigmore Hall. He is a past Chair of the South African Literary Journal, and the originator of the South African National Poetry Prize. He has published four collections — *the stretching of my sky*

(2018), *the shores of years* (2019), *beyond a distant edge* (2021) and *of clay* (2022). Instagram:@poetarchie

Abdullatif Khalid (Latif The Sacred Poet) is a male Ugandan passionate poet, an educator, writer, word crosser, scriptwriter, essayist, content creator, orator, public speaker and a word spoken artist currently doing a bachelor of arts with education in English and literature at mountains of the moon university. He offers creative writing services and do performs at projects focused on brand/campaign awareness, luncheons, date nights, product launches, concerts, festivals and many more. His poems have been featured in several poetry publications for example; "Best New African Poets 2022 ANTHOLOGY" "WRITING A WOMAN ANTHOLOGY: poetry and visual art vol. 3 – an anthology by Asian and African writers and artists" "Voice from My Roots" – a poetry collection by Dove Eye Poetry and "The Writers Space Africa, July 2023 magazine".

Ojonugwa John Attah is a Nigerian poet, story writer, phone photographer, tech enthusiast, and a member of the United People Global. He is a 2019 pioneer Ambassador of Teachers' Naija (a Teachers' Reality TV Show in Nigeria) and he is also a graduate of the 2011 Fidelity Bank International Creative Writing Workshop. His works have been published in and on: *Dreams at Dawn (An Anthology of short stories from the International Creative Writing Workshop series organized by Fidelity Bank Plc), Best New African Poets, Tush Stories, The Muse at Nsukka, Drumtide online Magazine (USA), FaithWriters, Saturday Sun newspaper (Nigeria), Kikwetu online journal.* He is @OJohnAttah on X (Formerly Twitter).

William Khalipwina Mpina is a poet, fiction writer, economist, and data analyst for the Malawi Revenue Authority. He has published his works in a large number of international journals and literary magazines, as well as in over ten local anthologies, including *Malawi: A Place Apart (2017)* by former Norwegian ambassador to Malawi AsbjØrn Eidhammer. Mpina did his university education at Chancellor College, University of Malawi in Zomba, where he was a member of the Chancellor College Writers Workshop between 2011 and 2015. He is a co-editor of *Walking the Battlefield, a bilingual poetry anthology on COVID-19,* and *Tilembe Newsletter of the Malawi Union of Academic and Non-Fiction Authors.* His books include *Mooning the Morning (2022),*

Princess from the Moon (2020), Shattered Dreams (2019), Blood Suckers (2019), Shadows of Death and other poems (2016), Namayeni (2009), and *Njiru (2003).* He is currently the treasurer general for the Malawi Union of Academic and Non-Fiction Authors. You can follow him on Twitter @MpinaWilliam.

Martin Chrispine Juwa is a History teacher and Poet based in Lilongwe, Malawi. His poetry is a raw dialogue around identity, the natural environment, poverty, mental health, education, violence, spiritual healing and political activism. His work appears widely in both local and international online and print journals, magazines and anthologies including three *BNAP Anthologies, The Poet Magazine, JAYL (Volume 2), Held Magazine, Orchards Journal, Southern Humanities Review, Libero America Journal, Pensive Journal of Spirituality, Last Girls Club, Daily Drunk, Afreecan Read, Griots of Ubuntu,* and many others. He has a debut poetry anthology titled *Drifting Smoke (2020).* Martin dreams of establishing an organization to support literary talent in Malawi.

Andrey B. Matambo is an award-winning Poet, born, raised, and based in Lusaka City. An Animal Scientist by profession, he spends most of his free hours reading and writing. He enjoys a broadspectrum of African and Jamaican music, some Country and a wee of the Sean-carter-era hiphop. In addition, Andrey likes swimming, watching movies, taking evening walks, working out, and walking his K9s or tending the garden. As part of his 'Places life-list', he hopes one day to visit Ghana and the Great Zimbabwe, and off the motherland, Deutschland.

Edward Dzonze has contributed to more than 20 other anthologies and poetry journals .His poetry is a counter-culture that have come to breathe life unto fading cultures. He lives in Harare's high density surburb of Budiriro. He have five poetry tittles to his name.

Chigozie Anariochi George popularly known by his pen name **Chisimdi George** is a poet and novelist.his works have appeared in literary anthologies which includes: The fifth Chinua Achebe poetry/essay anthology, the sixth Chinua Achebe poetry/ essay anthology, End SARS voices anthology of poems and essays against police brutality and battery, Anthology in honor of late professor Jerry agada, 11th woman scream international anthology, *Love Nwantinti(a* *special valentine poetry collection 4th edition)* , *MY VAL MY TONIC (a special valentine poetry collection 5th edition) Voices of Revolutions (a collections of poems/essays in recent happening in Nigeria), THE TRICK IS TO KEEP BREATHING (a covid19 stories from Africans and non American writers vol3), Best "NEW" African Poets 2022 ANTHOLOGY,* He is a graduate of University of Nigeria Nsukka, He is from Abia State Nigeria.

Adiela Akoo is an emerging South African poet. She is the founder and editor of The Quilled Ink Review literary journal. Her debut book, *Lost in a Quatrain*, was First Runner-Up for poetry in the South African Independent Publishers Awards 2021. She has also represented the Durban UNESCO City of Literature in various collaborations with other Cities of Literature and has volunteered her time as Vice Chair of the Literacy Association of South Africa, KZN, among other things. Find out more about her here: https://linktr.ee/Adiela.Akoo

My name is **Saba Dickson** from Nigeria. I am an aspiring story writer and a poet with hope of putting my emotions into writing.

Chenjerai Mhondera is a rabbi, the dissident reporter and Lord of Controversies. He is a citizen of the World. He is the author of *HURRICANE Tortures of Now (Zimbabwe), Hurricane To The World (Nigeria), Manifesto#Anthology of Peace (Nigeria), A Case of Love and Hate (Zimbabwe).* His works also appear in over forty publications; online journals and blogs, magazines and anthologies. Among the lot - including *Best New African Poets (BNAP) 2015 Anthology (Cameroon), BNAP 2016 Anthology, BNAP 2017 Anthology, BNAP 2018 Anthology, BNAP 2019 Anthology, BNAP 2020 Anthology, BNAP 2021 Anthology, BNAP 2022 Anthology.*

Antreka Tladi was born in Jane Furse, Limpopo, Republic of South Africa where he received his primary and secondary education and currently lives. His poems have been published in local and international journals and Anthologies including the *Avbob poetry project, the Otherwise Engaged literature and Art journal and the Calabash Literary journal.* He was honoured with an African Honoree Authors' Award in 2022.

Jabulani Mzinyathi is a poet, novelist born in 1965 in Gwelo in the then Rhodesia [now Zimbabwe]. He is an ex –teacher, ex-magistrate. Currently he is a lawyer in private practice. Jabulani is also a human capital management practitioner. He did several short courses in alternative dispute resolution, basics of international law, English for business and tourism, English language and literature, journalism, understanding environmental law, public relations, international relations, thesis writing, customer care and change management. Jabulani's published works are: *Under The Steel Yoke, Righteous Indignation, In The Steel Talons, Along The Way [poetry] and a chiShona novel entitled Mumambure.* He reads with 'self-punishing avidity'.

Joseph Daniel Sukali is a Malawian writer, poet, editor and mental health advocate. He is a Mzuzu University graduate and an employee of Emmanuel International Malawi besides being a Publications Officer for GrandPen Publications. Sukali is the author of *A Dance in the Mud (2023), Harnessing Inner Tranquillity (2021),* and *Dealing with a Heartbreak (2020),* and co-author of a poetry anthology *Whispers of Beating Hearts (2021).* He is working on a poetry anthology and mental health- Pan-African book with titles; "Aborted at Birth: Funeral of the Unborn" and "Sorry I'm not Sorry We are All Sick: Awakening Mental Reconfiguration" respectively.

Kennix Odera is a KENYAN published poet and a scholar of the Queen's language. His poems were published in Best New African Poets 2022 Anthology. He is a graduate with Bachelor of Education Arts, with Information Technology (English and Literature) from MASENO UNIVERSITY. His poetic justice flames from within the thrills and fangs of life. His love for poetry was obvious from his early school days but only started showcasing it in the recent years. He is a High School teacher of English and Literature in Kenya.

Philip Miti: I was born on December, 5 1991 in the city of Lusaka, capital of Zambia. My father abandoned me when I was one week old leaving Mom stranded with bills to settle. I was raised by my mother's ex-husband Mr Miti and my step siblings in Kabulonga. In 1998 Mr Miti passed away. In 2001 when I was 12 years old my mother took me and my immediate step elder brother Alick Miti as well my step sister's son Godfrey to stay with her in Makeni where she was working as a house maid for the Indians. In 2018 I went to University at Kwame Nkrumah University to study English and Civic Education in teaching. In 2020 when I was in third year of my degree program I dropped out School due to financial challenges. I'm now into business vending, selling good rising money so I maybe go back for further education.

Abigirl Phiri is a prolific Zimbabwean writer and poet. She has compiled and co-authored in various anthologies. Additionally, she believes when it comes to poetry sharing is tantamount to caring.

Adaobi Charlyn Chilekezi is a student of the English and Literary Students at the University of Nigeria. She has published her poems in anthologies and journals in and outside Nigeria, She is currently working on her first collection of poems.

Obinna Chilekezi is an insurance practitioner and writer. His poems and essays have appeared in journals and anthologies. His published works are *Songs of a Stranger at the Smiling Coast, My Gambian and Other poems, and Calligramme*. He has also written and published articles and books on insurance.

Adebayo Julius Oyenyen is my name. I am a young promising writer, who had authored two books- College feelings, Trauma, both published on amazon.

Lucas Lungu Jr hails from a priestly lineage, devoted to the New Apostolic Church Faith. He contributes his talents to an orchestra, wielding his skills as a proficient violinist. Beyond music, Lucas serves as a peer educator within the non-governmental organization D.R.E.A.M.S. He wears many hats as a debater, advocate, and ardent feminist. His journey into poetry commenced in 2019, and Lucas is renowned for his traditional African poetry, celebrating African culture and literature. In late January, he ventured into spoken word poetry, gracing Roman Catholic stages with his performances. Lucas has also penned dramatic poems and plays for numerous institutions, nurturing his artistic passion alongside fellow poets.

Salmista Cortês, pseudonym of Celestino João Campaxi, angolan nationality, residing in Africa-Angola-Luanda, bornon 02/26/1997; is a poet, singer, proofreader, editor, speaker, and mentor. Graduatedin Portuguese Language Teaching at Higher Pedagogical School of Bengo. His passion for literature comes from his adolescence. Cortês writes poetry, novels, films, short stories and thoughts. In the Literature career, Cortês participated with poetic texts in the Anthology *Best New African Poets 2022* and others concurses from Portugal, Brasil...

Okolo Chinua is a writer who writes for many reasons, the beauty of tomorrow being the foremost. Currently he lives and writes from the suburbs of Onitsha, Anambra State.

McLayode is a proud school teacher in great love with the Eternal Word and forever tickled by the fresh use of word and tongue. He likes to describe himself as a thinker and writer giving full poetic expression to God's world view in the world's culture.

Colleen Venter. South African. Took part in combined poetry/art event: Fusion of art in poetry "Visual Expressions Exhibition" presented by Scava (Southern Cape Association of Visual Arts) at George Museum in September 2023. Lives in George, Western Cape. Enjoys poetry, writing and drawing.

David Chasumba is an award-winning Zimbabwean Author and Poet. His debut short story collection, *The Mad Man on First Street and Other Short Stories*, won the NAMA (National Arts Merit Award) in 2023 for Outstanding First Creative Published Work in Zimbabwe. His short stories were published in four anthologies; A Bundle of Joy and Other Short Stories from Africa, Momaya Short Story Review: (Treasure) (2015), Small Worlds anthology- University of Brighton Literature Society (2014) and Reflections anthology by University of Brighton Literature Society (2015). His short story, Crossing the Rubicon, was longlisted for the Fish Publishing Short Story Competition (2013-14). He published four short stories with Kalahari Review. He has recently published three poems in Ipikai Poetry Journal and a poem, *There are still poets* in Mosi oa Tunya Review Issue 2. David has two MA degrees from University of Sussex and Canterbury Christ Church University. David lives in Bexhill on sea. X: @davidchasumba22

Womba Nakazwe: I am a 27 years old lady living in Livingstone Zambia. I am passionate about literature and poetry is my favorite genre. I enjoy reading and writing poems. My favorite poets are Maya Angelou and Edgar Allen Poe.

Wellington Nwogu is an African poet from the Niger Delta region of Nigeria. His creative works have in recent times been approved as reading texts for University, College of Education, and Polytechnic students in Nigeria. Nwogu holds a PhD in Literature, a Master of Arts (M.A) degree in Literature and a Bachelor of Education

Degree (B.ED) in English Studies. He has more than fifteen published works to his name. He is a member of the Association of Nigerian Authors, Nigeria Literary Society and so on.

Kimutai Kemboi Allan is a Kenyan writer residing in Nairobi. His works have been shortlisted for *"Our Stories Redefined Anthology for African Writing 2023 (Poetry Edition)"* while others appear in or are forthcoming in; Our Poetry Archive, the INK Babies Literary Magazine, Written Tales, African Global Networks (AGN), Ake Review, The Active Muse, The Writer's Space Africa, the Kalahari Review, the Naluubale Review, Writers Resist and Havik's 2020 Anthology (Homeward).

Tajudeen Muadh is a young poet from Osun State, Nigeria. His works have appeared or forthcoming in different literary magazines and journals such as Kalahari review, Wax Poetry, African poetry magazine, brittle paper, meniscus journal, icreatives review and elsewhere.

Prosper C. Ìféányí writes from Lagos, Nigeria. His works are featured or forthcoming in Black Warrior Review, New Delta Review, Salt Hill, The Offing, Indianapolis Review, South Dakota Review, Magma Poetry, Westchester Review, and elsewhere. His microchapbook is *Sermon* (Ghost City Press, 2023).

Onatola Abiodun is from Ikenne Remo in Ogun State Nigeria. He is a published creative writer across genres of Literature. He lives, Study and write from Ibadan, Oyo State Nigeria.

MK Kuol is a "deliberate" surrealist whose work, while it is a mere dive into his subconscious mind, is closely reexamined in passionate rewriting. He delights in reading anything readable as well.

AFONSO KUDISSADILA, estudante Universitário no curso de Ciências Farmacêuticas, ingressou oficialmente nos mares da literatura em 2021, após participar da ANTOLOGIA POÉTICA : ESPERANÇAS PERDIDAS (BANCADA dos Escritores), e estreou mais na COLETÂNEA DONNA: VOZES QUE ECOAM (DA IRDE EDITORA), CL o marco da sua carreira literária, em 2022, foi seleccionado na para a 3ª. Edição da ANTOLOGIA POÉTICA EM HOMENAGEM AOS HERÓIS DE 4 DE FEVEREIRO.

Armando Botelho é o pseudónimo de Pedro Angelina Armando, nasceu aos 21 de Novembro de 2000, natural do Soyo/Zaire. Tentando ser escritor e poeta. Estudou Língua Portuguesa e E.M.C no ensino médio, na Escola de Formação de Professores do Soyo (EFP), actualmente conhecida como Escola do Magistério do Soyo (EMS) de 2016-2019. É estudante de Relações Internacionais na Universidade de Belas. É membro do Movimento Literragris e da Associação Nacional dos Estudantes de Relações Internacionais (ANERI).

DESTINO VENTURA, natural da Província do Zaire, município do Tomboco, membro do Círculo de Estudos Literários e Linguísticos Litteragris- CE3L, estudante de Relações Internacionais, na Universidade de Belas. Escritor e Crítico literário, tem textos de poesia publicados na Antologia Fio da Palavra (2018); Antologia Nós e Poesia (2019). Textos de crítica literária publicada na Mayombe- Revista Angolana de Crítica Literária (2021, 1º edição) e (2022, 2º edição).

Dnaffe Medina é pseudónimo de Medina Jorge, natural de Nzetu, província do Zaire. É poeta, professor e estudante de Sociologia no Instituto Superior de Ciências da Educação/ISCED – Luanda.

Hélder Simbad é poeta. Em muitos casos, é professor não assalariado; quando quer irritar os outros, gosta de brincar de crítico literário. Não é um gajo muito sério, mas venceu o prémio literário António Jacinto 2017 com a obra Enviesada Rosa. Como o presente livro é de poesia apenas, publicou também o livro Insurreição dos Signos e mais nada. O resto é zunga.

Henriques Fortuna nasceu no Ebo, Cuanza-Sul, é professor de Língua Portuguesa no Complexo Escolar Dr. Américo Boa Vida do Ebo, desde 2020, estudou Língua Portuguesa e Literatura no Ensino Médio, na Escola de Formação de Professores do Cuanza-Sul — Magistério do Sumbe —, andou no ISCED-Luanda em 2017 e 2018, no Curso de Ensino da Língua Portuguesa, é membro da Oficina Literária, criada pelo escritor Gociante Patissa, participou em duas Colectâneas de poesia — *Palavras São Tantas*, 2019, e *Versos de Lírios*, 2022 —. Escreve desde cedo, seus textos passaram a ser conhecidos ao assinar a rubrica de crónicas e sugestões de leituras na Rádio Kwanza-Sul, em 2015 e 2016. É o idealizador do club de leituras *"BAR DO LIVRO"*, com sede no Ebo.

Isabel Sango é natural de Maquela do Zombo, província de Uíge. É Escritora e jornalista. Marcou os primeiros passos no grupo teatral Jovens da Mulemba, tendo a posterior enveredado para a Escrita actuando como co-autora do poemário Vivências Paralelas, junto do escritor Antônio José Alçada. Sango é Estudante de Gestão de Empresas e Delegada Provincial da Brigada Jovem de Literatura de Angola, bem como Directora de Marketing da Associação dos jovens Escritores de Angola- AJEA. Das suas viagens artísticas, participou de Antologias como: Diário de uma quarentena(2020), Tanto Mar Entre Nós (Brasil,2021), Kandongueiros II (2021,) Antologia feminina pétalas e pedaços de nós, Poesias no Muro, entre outros.. Venceu o prêmio de literatura " Arco-Íris", e o prémio super fã da Record Tv.

João Horácio Alexandrino
Pseudônimo literário João O Pensador, é um poeta e romancista, designer gráfico, CEO da "Editora Mundo da Leitura.
Nasceu no dia 04 de abril de 2000, na Província da Huíla, filho de José Manuel Alexandrino, e de Aldina Josefa Alexandrino.

Sempre foi amante da literatura aprofundou ainda mais sobre o mundo da poesia e nele se encontrou. Tem como inspiração António Jacinto, Pepetela, José Saramago, José Eduardo Agualusa, Fernando Pessoa, ONDJAKI.

Khilson Khalunga nasceu nas terras de Angola aos 24 de Dezembro, amante das Letras e licenciado em Línguas e Literaturas Africanas pela Faculdade de Humanidades da Universidade Agostinho Neto. Tem texto publicado na Revista Palavra & Arte; é colunista residente do jornal O País. Participou da Antologia de crónica "Crónica das arruaças no país das maravilhas".

Luís Kapemba É pseudónimo literário de Luís Rodrigues Pinto Jerónimo. Desabrochou-se ao mundo no dia 28 de Abril de 1997, em Angola-Luanda, onde actualmente reside. É Desenhador Projectista, membro co-fundador do clube de leitura com matriz africana "Aldeia Sankhofa" e, também, membro do núcleo literário denominado "Centro Linguístico i Literário". Em 2018, participou da antologia poética "Nós e a Poesia", em homenagem ao mestre João Tala. Em 2020, participou da colectânea poética "(Uni)Versos dispersos ", organizado pela revista Palavra&Arte. Em 2022, fez parte da Antologia poética "Melhores Novos Poetas de África".

Maria Manuel Godinho Azancot de Menezes, filha de Manuel Pedro Azancot de Menezes e de Maria de Lourdes Pires Godinho, é mãe, avó e Pediatra. Vive em Angola desde a sua infância.Publicou 101 poemas no livro "Lua Mágica" e 102 poemas no livro "Voo Colorido"; participou em várias Antologias Portuguesas, no Libero America-Africa Journal, no Best New Africain Poets (2017, 2018, 2019, 2020, 2021,2022).

Mwene XI, pseudônimo de Jelson Bartolomeu Manuel Calunga, também conhecido por Sandro ou ainda Sandro Kalunga, nome que usa nas redes sociais. É estudante finalista do curso de psicologia do trabalho e das Organizações pela Faculdade de Ciências Sociais da Universidade Agostinho Neto em Luanda, Angola, país onde nasceu e onde reside.

Ntony Kunsevi, Yembe, Ex. Poeta das Calças Rasgadas, há 41 anos, surgiu das outras eras aos 8 desejos de Dezembro de dois seres, Paulo Kunsevi e Jorgina António Jacinto, nas verdejantes campos da terra de Kongo dya Ntotela, Zaire-Nzeto. Leitor que escreve poemas, crónicas, contos e outros textos ainda não classificados; Cidadão do universo com os pés firmes em Angola.

Satchonga Tchiwale, nasceu em Angola, Província do Bié. É Membro do Movimento Literário Litteragris. 2017, Venceu o concurso de declamação na Tv Zimbo, em homenagem ao poeta maior Agostinho Neto; Participou em várias antologias como: Antologia Internacional "Países da CPLP" POESIA DO FADO E DOS TAMBORES "5ª Edição, 2018";Revista TUNDA VALA II – Movimento Litteragris "3ª Edição, 2018"; Antologia em homenagem ao escritor João Tala "NÓS E A POESIA" "1ª Edição, 2019". Satchonga Tchiwale é Escritor, Poeta-Declamador, Editor de livro, Diagramador, Capista, Design Gráfico, Bailarino, Actor e Desenhista.

Simão Nzombo Antônio. Nasceu nas Ingombota, Luanda. aos 12 de junho de 1978.. funcionário no sector privado. Construção civil. Empreendedor. Tem na literatura, influências trazidas pela cultura hip-hop. Poenta e declamador em tempo livre. É membro do levart

Angola. co-fundador do Levart sector Cazenga.. Estreia com textos publicados nesta antologia

Vítor Ricardo: Nascido aos 28 de Janeiro de 1989 na Maternidade Augusto Ngangula em Luanda. Morador da comuna do Neves Bendinha, Município do Kilamba Kiaxi – Luanda. Formado em Contabilidade e Auditoria – Universidade Agostinho Neto. Estudante do curso de Gestão Bancaria e Seguros – ISAF. Comecei a escrever em 2006 (poemas). Em 2014 passei a envolver-me mais com a escrita dedicando mais tempo a ela. Sempre escrevendo poemas e algumas reflexões. Quatro livros publicados: *Miradouro da Lua – 2019; Cartas à Ana Cármen – 2021; Nzoji – Sonhos mutilados e Avessos de um Natal, lançados em 2022(E-book)*. Certificado de mérito da Fundação Arte e Cultura, num recital onde o livro "Miradouro da Lua" foi homenageado, isto aos 29 de Janeiro de 2020.

Né le 10 avril 2002 à Ekondo-Titi, Sud-ouest du Cameroun, **Yves Laroche Ngodjo Abata** est un étudiant camerounais, vivant et y poursuivant ses études à l'université de Yaoundé 1titulaire d'une licence en langue et linguistique espagnole.

Arnold Mondo K. est un poète, écrivain congolais, né le 28 février 1992 à Kinshasa, capitale de la République Démocratique du Congo. Il est diplômé en latin-philosophie et licencié en Relations internationales. Amoureux de la science et de la littérature, il est auteur de plusieurs poèmes. Sa passion pour la poésie date depuis son enfance. Il a participé à plusieurs concours scolaires de poésie et contribué à l'anthologie des Meilleurs Nouveaux Poètes Africains, BNAP, 2022.

Michel Dongmo Evina se passionne d'écriture et de poésie depuis une décennie. Sa plume se nourrit de rencontres, du Cameroun son biotope naturel, et de l'héritage des anciens. Ses textes sont publiés dans plusieurs anthologies, notamment « Le Crépuscule des âmes sœurs » et « Bearing Witnesss » (2020).

Faustin Junior Embolo Embolo est un Camerounais dont, la plume commence à marquer les esprits. Ayant atteint l'âge de la « parole », il surfe allègrement entre révolte poétique et panafricanisme. L'amour pour sa terre favorise l'éclosion d'une pensée rationnelle. Plongé dans un univers hostile, le Cameroun demeure jusqu'au sang sa patrie, un pays dont, la densité culturelle a joué en faveur de la réalisation de cette œuvre. Etudiant à la faculté de philosophie de l'Université de Yaoundé I et à la faculté de droit à l'Université de Yaoundé II en cycle recherche, l'auteur porte en lui l'espérance d'une jeunesse en quête de model.

Mbonyi Corneille est né le 31 janvier 2008 en République démocratique du Congo, plus précisément à Goma. À travers l'encre de sa plume, il s'efforce à donner vie aux mots en explorant une multitude de thèmes. Sa poésie est un reflet de sa sensibilité et de sa vision du monde, offrant des perspectives riches et nuancées sur ces sujets cruciaux.

Serge BILLO EBANGA est né à Ngaoundere dans le Grand-nord, Cameroun au début des années 80. Ce passionné de littérature est auteur de plusieurs recueils. Membre de *World Poetry Movement-*Cameroon (WPM) et du collectif des auteurs africain (CODAAF), il est, depuis janvier 2023, ambassadeur de l'Association des Poètes africains (APA) au Cameroun.

Introduction

From 2015 upto 2023 we have been able to issue out, yearly, an anthology of Africa poets, through 9 years of publishing this beautiful anthology of the best contemporary African poets and in the process we have published and archived over 1000 African poets. And this year without fail we offer you *Best New African Poets 2023 Anthology* which comprises of several dozens of African poets from the Portuguese, English and French speaking African countries. We expect the anthology to continue into another decade but also to seed into other forms of poetic expressions starting from next year. We intent to work on *Best New African Poets International Festival of the Arts*, an event that will bring together all these poets we have been able to publish the last 9 years to showcase their talent in a week of festivities in Harare, Zimbabwe. Those who would love to help us or sponsor us in this new endevour can get in touch with us on the emails on the title page.

This year's anthology has poems that covers the usual gamut of issues: love, unrequited feelings, relationships, death, poetry making, politics, and we were excited to see Mashigo tackling the ongoing Israel/ Hamas war, and the ill-treatment of the Palestinian people for generations under the Israeli government, culture, religion, spirituality, identity, belonging, memory, individuality and all sorts of other existential dilemmas that the young African poets deal with day to day.

And as per our tradition since 2016 we allowed and took the poets through 4 collaborations this year, the first is on witchcraft, the second dealt with the erotic poem, the third is on the effects of AI on African writing landscape and the last dealt with the reorganization of world politics in relation to the Ukrainian war and the incoming multipolar world view we seem set on.

Another important thing we have done is to give space to poetics. In this anthology we have the former contributors of the anthology interviewing one of the editors, Tendai Rinos Mwanaka, who has been with the anthology from conception all through the years and also as the editor of the English entries and publisher of the anthology.

We welcome you all to *Best New African Poets 2023 Anthology* and hope you will enjoy this beautiful poetic journey.

POETRY
Aminu Femi Jamiu

Poetry is deeper than you know
It flows like an ocean
Vast like the universe
Here am I
In Her path of immortality
Sailing and sinking in metaphor
As simile smile ironically
At the waves that hunch back
That ushered my arrival
But nature weaved me in a poem
Out of her cosmic pot
To be sung as a lullaby
Laying the Sun
And the Moon to rest
In this literary sky
I'd sail like an eagle
Soar deeper into the ether
Breathe the breath of poetry
Till I lay my golden quill
On the lap of nature.

SOUL
Aminu Femi Jamiu

Soul is immortal
She's is part of nature
Soul do travel
Give yours a wing
Let her flee with nature
To wander above the hills
And soar beyond the highest heaven
Let her sail along with the gentle breeze
Through the depth of the ocean
Feel the breath of the mother-Earth
And dance the fantasy of this universe
To bring thee tales and wisdom of ages
For soul can sing the songs of nature
Soul is immortal
Soul do travel
Give yours a wing
She's part of nature
Ready to sail forever.

WE ARE HUMANS TOO
Aminu Femi Jamiu

We are not as fortunate
Just as your kids
No inheritance
And formal education
To gain our liberty

When the scorching sun
Burn like hell
When the rain beats
Like bullets on the roof
And when it storms

Throughout the night
We are there trudging the labyrinth of paths
For we lack an abode
To lay our heads
Each day seeking

For a place to rest
With empty bowel
Off we set to beg for alms
Stopping passersby and strangers
Just for little food
To feed ourselves

With tattered attire
Designed with parching treads
Many keep despising us
Refusing to offer us bread
Thinking we are not human

To them, we are only beggars
Who have no vision
Hope and aspiration

As they give us no attention
Just because of our shabby nature
And sun tanned face

Though we are beggars
Just because we are orphans
Cheated by Nature
So stop despising us
For we are humans too.

Dedicated to all ORPHANS.

INE NDEPAPA
Austin Kaluba

Ine ndepapa.
bacilende baleupwa,
banacisungu baleikala abashimbe.
Ine ndepapa.
Ifipuba fileitila umuto,
impanda shiletobela panshi.
Abashakwate ☐ ombe ebalenwa umukaka,
kacema alenwa amenshi.
Ine ndepapa.
Abalwani babuntunse ebaleteka,
nokupingula imilandu.
Ine ndepapa.
ubufi bulebunsha cishinka,
nokucisalile ciibi.
Isonde liletatakwila Barabbas,
lyatanika Yesu.

IT SURPRISES ME (English translation)
Austin Kaluba

It surprises me
To see immoral women getting married
While virgins remain unmarried.
It surprises me
To see fools outwitting the wise.
I see those without cows drinking milk;
while the herdboy drinks water
It surprises me
To see enemies of humanity,
ruling and judging
It surprises me
to see lies drowning the truth.
Closing the door in its face.
The whole world is applauding Barabbas
and crucifying Jesus.

ABASUNGU BANEMBO
Austin Kaluba

Mwebasungu banembo
Ababutuka ubwikele,
Abapata umwela wakumwenu.
Mwebasungu banembo
Abasendwa nakankungwe wafyabene
Abapepa imilingu imbi.

Shibweleniko panono.
Mwebasungu banembo
Abalwala amalwele yabukatubi
Ababekela mukupepa imfuba shimbi.
Fumeni pacintamba mwaninapo
Fuleni nefilundu fyabene ifyo mwafwala

WHITES WITH INCISIONS (English translation)
Austin Kaluba

You whites with incisions
Who run while seated.
You hate the wind in your country.
You whites with incisions
Who worship foreign gods
Blown away by the foreign whirlwind.

Come down to earth
You who die from glutton-related diseases;
bowing before foreign shrines.
Come down from the pedestal
Take off the foreign garbs you adorn.

INSEKU
Austin Kaluba

Akapumpu kacipuba katwala mukukumbatila umwana wamfumu.
Nokusekwila inseku ecileta ubusomboshi bwampomfu
Ubukali bwabufyashi, ebuleta ubuntunse.
Iŋombe yabula umucila, ilatalalika umutima wakwa Lesa.
Pantu inseku na male fimo
Ngefyo ukulila Eloi Eloi, lipusukilo lya muntu.
Ishibeni nokuti ubucindami bwakwakapingula wamilandu bufuma kuli kabolala
Incende ikulapo icetemwiko, imo ine napamena ulupato.
Bucilalelale bwe hule cimo cine bobucende bwawaupwa
Kanshi mwitemwa ingo mupate umucila
Pantu imbola shanshimu, buci ubwalowa.
Nemfwa, yakwatafye ulubola lumo.

WEEDS (English translation)
Austin Kaluba

A persistent fool can woo a princess.
Remember that weeding leads to a bountiful harvest.
And it is labour pains that bring life.
A tail-less cow softens God's heart.
Because weeds and desired crops are the same
Remember crying Eloi Eloi is man's salvation
Just as the dignity of a judge comes from the criminal
Because the source of love and hate is the same.
The love making of a wife is no different from that of a whore
So don't love the leopard and hate its tail
Because the stings of a bee is sweet honey
And death has only one sting.

Dear Golden Eyed Lady
Abbas Muhammad Usman

This is not a Poem
But the atom from
The bounty of calm
Enclosed in you.

The serenity is synonym
Of your golden name which
Painted in colors of green
Of nature of autumn.

I am blessed to have you.
You are the gift from Jalla
To me, who was lost in the
Black desert of nowhere.

Your smiling face resemble
The rain in a loneliest desert.
Your voice resemble the
Blanket in the midst of glacier.

Through your voice nature
Whisper to humanity, the
Melody in your voice moist
With calm is abode to peace.

Dear golden eyed lady
With dazzling raven skin
Which symbolizes the pride
Of our ancestors, give me
Single smile sailed straight
From your heart, for that
Is the greatest gift ever.

Missive To Saharan Princess
Abbas Muhammad Usman

Oh! The beautiful angel
Of prettiness & benevolence,
Understand my wailing heart.
My libs can't utter these words,
They are heavy. Time is going on.
My pen is decimated before
Your kingdom of beauty.
How I could tell you?

Oh! The black-beauty queen
These are the poet's words
That can not be said to anyone
But you. Let's be the neighboring
Stars and twinkle together
I don't know, but if these heavy
Words drag this poet into a grave,
Do ask my close friends
About my hidden secrets

Oh! The golden-eyed black queen.
Even if these are my last words
Let be known that, I like your
Ebony type skin. I like your smile.
I adore your calmness. Trapped.
Understand the language
Of my tendered soul, oh! Princess.
Tell me when my soul will
Measure a sky with its wing again?

The Secret
Abbas Muhammad Usman

I closed my eyes
To exploit the secrets
Of essence, I see nothing
But your face. I see peace in
Your eyes. Comfort in your lips.
I choose to be brightest star
Twinkling beside you

You are the secret of
Earth, gold of nature
And conquerors' extol;
They conquered, onslaught
And destroyed cities to win
Your grin. Undaunted.
Halcyon I remain.

You are the secret of
Contentment, calmness,
Mark of serenity
And smile of the sea;
Who embellished her shores
With gold and salt of heaven.
I am nothing but glint
Of the secret.

The sightseer
Lucas Zulu

Sometimes a warbler wings its way from the western.
Sometimes with a feather, sometimes with a binocular.
Sometimes tied in with a camera and take pictures
of familiar landmarks, like a tallest tower in *Joburg* skyline,
fond of flights as they conjure up pleasant memories
tinge with blues, ahead of him was a cloud of anxiety
after the chap ogled an iron-bird crash on the alpine region.
Flying stirred uncomfortable emotions within his bosom.
However, he did not want to live on his nerves,
maybe in want for a nerve to fly again. As the kite takeoff,
a big man with big eyes and big ears. He muttered
you know what, above *Maboneng* skyscrapers,
there are no borders simply bleached puffy clouds
and so whatever happens in the *aviation* history,
the *aviators* are always on the wing. This is how they live,
this is how they survive; this is how they carry the day.

Four by Four
Lucas Zulu

As the eagles awakens me with a scream,
as the first light imbued the skies with sublime
pastels of dawn. As the geese cackles above me
on this rustic route, there's no silver wheels
except me, on a sandy road between the dunes
for a century in a quasi-Dakar Rally, as a trail
might say, I have a strong desire to travel.
Then comes a herd of moo without a herdsman.
I sound the horn but the brown cattle's
refuse to haul off and begin to move off jerkily
like a hee-haw. These are blue days oozing a whiff
of argh! And I am about to give myself to haze.
So to speak I crave to find a way out of its maze,
I grit my teeth and carry on in thick clag,
without a tow-truck to haul me out of the sand
sometimes I'd wish if I was a Boing airplane
I'd pass over the bog that stand on my path
but then not born with eagles. So I stare at every
monolithic impediment as a little hiccup. The sun
split its sides sniggering as stumbling blocks
sought to snag, its ray's peek through the mist
only the sun's yolk sees a lot of sand in me.
Audacity has salvaged me like a spare wheel.

Beyond the War
Oladele Babajamu

Beyond the war
Remains the wards
With the scars
And nothing to cover

The land is drained
From the barren earth
The sun scorches on the indebted land
Nothing left for Mother Earth

Everyone is restless
Like the bird that perches
On a dangling rope
Everywhere remains tense

There's neither rain
Nor grain on the land
The farmer must pray for rain
In order to eat grain

The men remain lean
The women become flat chested
With strands of boney buttocks
And famished children

No villain and no valour- man
No victor and no Vanquished
No winner and no loser
Everyone remains a champion
Champions in their own domain

THIS IS OUR TIME
Oladele Babajamu

This is our to take dance steps
To rhyme with the trumpet sound of progress
A time to listen to the clanging cymbals of
Our great ancestral rhythms

A time to remain focused on our imagined feature
As we take a picture of our glorious future
With a rainbow of creative literature
To fabricate our holistic scripture

This is our time for renaissance
To turn our imaginations to realities
A time to turn opportunities to possibilities
And to advance and make waves

It's our time to turn the tide
As we take the bounties of our heritage
And march on with our imaginations
To create our dream nation

This is our time to take our destiny
And scheme into the scheme of things
As we savour our heritage for a sustainable rhythm
To prevent a dance of death by our future generations

THE BOAT OF LIFE
Oladele Babajamu

The Boat of life
Rocking away
Out of the way
In undulation motion

Too many captains
Without visions
Nor technocrat
Everywhere is tense
Its survival of the fittest
For the masses on the Boat
Irrespective of races
Or idiosyncrasies
Everyone's struggling and smiling
For a glorious voyage
On the curling and over falling waves

PREDATOR STILL ROAMS AROUND
Geraldo Bleza Malota

In the wee moments of 1964, we thought we had defeated the selfish colonisers
But till now, their sons and daughters continue to exert their powers
Ours is a sorry site for we are brainwashed with alien indoctrinations of the masters
For we only look helplessly and stand aside
Our hands are too paralysed to halt the monsters
We are witnessing a colonization worst for our age
Unfortunately, we have reciprocated it as the order of the day
We gaze as we stab each other's backs
We remain mute as selfish and power-hungry individuals loot the little we have
We just remain silent as the greedy souls build empires in our slums
Ours is weeping when thieves rob us the little we toil for in the name of religious obligations
Big shoes of the more privileged step on our heads as we trade our little paths
We continue to be pinned as we dance in the reverberating rhythms of weak minds
We are not done yet! We thought the oppressor had gone but his recapitulations still roam around!

THAT LUCK CHARM
Geraldo Bleza Malota

My ears danced gladly when I heard that "hard works pays off"
My heart thumped with inexplicable joy when I was told that "education is the key to success"
I innocently waited for my own "Mama I made it" moments for I grew up believing that patience unlocks bigger achievements
I worked smarter and with so much dog effort as I was programmed.

But look at me now, my life is a total mess
I am blurred in total tatters
My academic books have become a darling habitat for unruly spiders
My own papers are now smeared with the stubborn *katondo* dust
I shed tears when I look back and see how my tedious journey has been a pointless *Mfecane*
All dreams shattered, efforts unappreciated and aspirations drowned.

I now know I was swimming in a silent pool of great illusions
Pain has consistently stabbed my heart
As is struggle to bear the insults of the mob and make ends meet
My candle was burnt on both ends
Indeed, ours is a hollow full of empty expectations.

Am gutted down with sorrow
My eyes never dosed off from my Bible
As I read with optimism that "God blesses his faithful while they slumber"
Now am just a little useless fellow in a broken world's abyss
I never got fatigued with hearing the loud noises of enthusiastic motivational speakers.

Then fate whispered painful sentiments to me: "Hold on lad!"
The horns of life put me at my proper humble pew as I ate my own share of the bitter cake
Yes as bad luck taught me the necessity of chance in this our crazy cosmos

I tried everything I could to escape this tragedy
I kissed every face of life to be happy
But here I am, devastated to the core
This is why I just need a luck charm now
As I pen these cries of a sad African youth weeping deep within: "this is our untold story!!"

AFRICA DON'T BLINK
Geraldo Bleza Malota

I hail from the Mighty Africa
I am black and proudly African
A true gigantic seed from the continent's Warm Heart
Neither existing here by chance nor by choice but mere necessity.

Africa! We are one race
Though torn apart through our physical boarders
Which aggravate the uncalled-for feuds
Brought by demoralized unrealists with their unprecedented antagonisms.

We stumble, stagger and fall
As "foreigners" salivate over our captivating resources
Their insatiable appetites gnaw our adorable treasures
So anxious to drink to drink all our wealth their unquenchable thirst and to feast over us all with their burning desires.

When all their excessive expectations collapse
The Westerners brand our rituals and activities as ungodly
While they try to cripple our economies
Salivating to mercilessly devour us.

Mother Africa sobs as the foreigners rob us
They disband our unity to keep us at recurring war
They charge "faith groups" to continue arguing while they polish up our minerals
They brainwash us and misguide our education systems just to fit in theirs and impose their Western supremacy
O gosh! As my poor Africa lies in state: done and silted with silted culture.

Surely, we can save and serve Africa
Yes, we have a "vampire in the city"
Cockroaches and armyworms have encroached our vicinity

Look at me and answer my questions: Since when did Africa become a dumping site? Is Africa a dust bin? Is Africa a testing lab?

We are at war
A huge battle to re-awaken our colourful dreams
A tussle against our manipulated thoughts
A fight to regain our controlled ideas.

We march on into this battle and we don't sleep
To watch encroachers blood over our latent successes
Africa don't blink a while
Lest we continue clapping for the West in our backyard as we dance to their own tunes.

We watch helplessly as they facet our cultural values
We are one big village and we will triumph and resurrect our smiles again
Our victory songs shall ricochet powerfully in their ears
As we reap the grain of our painfully sown dream
So stay awake Africa and don't blink!

Made in the oven
Justice Masangano

As adversity progresses the chariots of time heals our broken soul
Despite the muscle dealt a big blow still we rise and stand tall
Hurt whole by the hard trial so thick our skin grow that we sparkle more
However foul the torment we celebrate the stars of every score
Both in sunshine and snow we are always ready to flow
Finding beauty as the epitome of our objective call
To be vigilant in the battle and win the war as our goal
Watching every obstacle fall.

I call it my freedom
Justice Masangano

Once I wake up
To the sweet songs in my ear
Sounds the deaf can almost hear
Mesmerizing beats and rhythms of birds floating the air
Whistling deep poetry in amazing solidarity
Sang with passion and mind-tingling simplicity
The verses oozing with immeasurable dexterity
Patching the wounds of yesterday's agony
I call it my freedom

The sun, meanwhile
Indispensable in its visibility
Its soothing hues a pleasant structure
Gold and rubies sparkling the horizon
Making a huge creative picture
Igniting silhouettes of hope
Reimbursing the faith once blurred
As the wet breeze filters into my room
Carrying the smell of sweet-scented flowers
I shout praise to the invincible one
I call it my freedom.

The future
Justice Masangano

Its night
I am sitting on the verandah of my mountain top house
Gazing the silent city
It looks green in the darkness
As the color of its atmosphere
It's creepy, but fascinating in a way sort of
It pulls the valves of my heart
Makes worms craw under the coat of my skin
Lightning never cease to crack, so is thunder
Its telephone lines touches the skies
I hear avatars live there
And no human being trespasses it
Perhaps this place exist in the future

Dream of Desperation
Alshaad Kara

The desire to love
Is a miracle spree,
Down the anguish
Of one's own envy.

It's more than giving
Forward to a passionate
Release,
It is to let go of anything
Conformist

And throw yourself
To a completely new
Spiritual adventure
With no regression.

Spirit of the Heart
Alshaad Kara

It hurts hard in the guts,
When love makes you
A fool...

The darkness at heart
Is the silence
Of your affection...

Heal the tempest
In your eyes,

And you shall feel
The feelings
Become
Void...

The pain in the heart
Is the fear of anger

That makes the
Spirit of the heart.

Men of Africa
Alshaad Kara

Beat the soil,
Run through this turmoil,

They, who appears at sunrise...
They, who appears at sunset...

Shall set a foot
On the floor of Elysium...

Spill that bloody heart,
Which bear the beatings
Of the beadings,

Since beauty is in the savannah,
Blooming the sunset of love!

THIS NIGHT IS A HALLOWEEN NIGHT
Emmanuel Douglas Mulomole

This night is a really halloween night
Its nefarious spirit has embraced me so tight
In me all fears waking up suddenly
Something jumping and disappearing regularly
For sure, it is the witches action is dancing
Carefully I heard a voice that monster is shouting

This night is a truly Halloween night
All my dreams has drowned in ghost shadow light
In my naked eyes has seen, the black cat screaming
And ghoulish whistle has called an owl start hooting
Leading everything in me thru the witches darkness
Keeping October end with the genuine frightfulness

THE RECONCILIATORY VOICE
Emmanuel Douglas Mulomole

Gleam the metaphors of unadulterated truth
Helps all the generations from youth to youth
With the really profoundest proverb of peace
As a instrument of sweetly reconciliatory voice
Oneness allures the blessings from above father
Through the verisimilar voice of reconcilers
A clarion call brings us in shell of togetherness
Reflect the bright light of pristine lovableness
Make the splendiferous colours like rainbow
Turn up all colours in common purpose of bow
As to welcome peace in our family and nation
Let us stand on the triumph of reconciliation
To fight against direct or indirect segregation
To win the epochal voice of no confrontation
To shun the guffaw of the act of retaliation
Let reconciliatory voice to embrace our life
Envision the future to hold a tranquil plumage
To evince the spirited respectability to all ages
Let us beam the reconciliatory voice so lovely
Bring the peerless light in family, nation brightly
Enliven all the real spirit in winsome wisdom
Bury, forget all grudges with harmonic loom
Spread the messages of lovable consistence
In all the forms of rarely opulent sustenance
Bestow a realness of mighty on us with rapture
Through consummate love to relational structure
Considerable calm creates a blissful living
Often retains our life with peaceful song
As a poem reciting a lovely stanza of glee
Flow amicably into the heart of nurturing
Reconciliatory voice gleams a forgiveness
As a lofty loom of chasing the contentions.

THE STRENGTH OF HOPE
Emmanuel Douglas Mulomole

We are very young than the longest tale of hope
Our dearest mother always tell us about the strength of hope
Hope is lovely and wonderful than an extreme fears
A brightly reflective light is in hope that always bear.

Hope has the wings like the splendiferous butterfly
Helps us to fly with a pure endurance so patiently
Until a rare liberty of hope will shine like a bright sun
With a wonderful and hopeful smile not a callous fun.

Hope is like a journey which is full optimistic expectations
In its way, like bird sings its wordless tune in all situations
Showing the preaching about the soul to stay in regardless obstacles
But, it helps our devastated souls to regain their grandeur of senses.

Hope is a profoundest beacon of light in the storm
Always help us to survive the tests and trials of our life
Hope always enjoy and excite in the lovely and humble hearts
That liberates us from despair, gives us the strength to move on.

EPICEDIUM
Emmanuel Tumwesige

We shall meet in that valley
Where skulls are given life
Through darkness in a gloomy journey
To the weariness of committed vile
Of our Africa.
Laid by your ribs are sheets of pain
And a cushion a stone of unsettled plans
Of deposing unpopular chiefs of the plain
Who rambunctiously took your pride,
Our Africa.
Laid to rest though in the bosom of your friends
Lies hope of your resurrection in grace
All the hyphy chiefs will yelp
And Africa shall gale.

THE DIFFERENT SIMILARITY
Emmanuel Tumwesige

My friend wants things to change,
But from what to what?
Sugar to salt
Or salt to sugar?

My friend, don't insist
Everything is on a script
To be like this
Or like that.

Men act like men
Women act like women
have you checked
Between your legs?

Can we share genitals?
Is it a fight of genitals?
Or one to draw
Close to another?

My friend, a spear
Will never collect water
Nor can a pot hunt,
Vitality stares differently.

When man stretches angrily
Woman softens joyously
To let him in
To cool hopefully.

My friend, vitality stares differently
What is kept between the thighs
Work differently
To make ties.

What if a mortar is the pestle
And the pestle the mortar!
- nuts would dance.
What if the woman impregnates
And the man impregnated!
- oh! the balloon knot would wail.

My friend, let the fire cease,
Balancing exists
Sugar is for sweetness
And salt for sweetness.
A number added to another
Doesn't assume the other
But purposeful
In changing the look.

Let the man be
Let the woman be
All take different paths
Walking the same journey
All on each ones' shoulder pat
All days of their journey
Let things run by the supreme script.

I MISS YOU
Emmanuel Tumwesige

Walking up and down the streets
Checking through my veins and muscles
To get that little thing that could give me a clue.
Staggering wandering as my soul fails and weeps
All the poems you wrote are just but bundles
Let me know when you'll come back I will be waiting at the brook.

Through my shelf I search for your hand
I feel the love in the lines you wrote
This brings back the pain of the moment you left;
I am maimed by this memory and I beg you return
before I lose the remaining drop of blood.
But even so when I am breathing my last
I will let you know how much I longed for you,
And now I am camping in the cold as I wait for you at the brook.
And I got flies to talk wishing to see your feet at the bank.
My love, I miss you

THE WIND BRINGS SONGS
Emman Usman Shehu

The wind needs no tongues
to sing its variety of songs

leaving it to the listener
to decipher the context.
The wind sings songs

needing no dancer
to be the interpreter.
The wind brings songs

like an orchestra
without tongues.

WHY DO THEY SAY THE DAY BREAKS ?
Emman Usman Shehu

Why do they say the day breaks
when it is not as fragile

as an egg and the sun
that follows is not a yolk ?

All it does is slowly show
like a nyctinastic plant
the glory of the morning

no matter what had taken place
the day before the morning.

SEASON'S EXTRACT
Emman Usman Shehu

In a season's syllabus extract
rain talks tense switch to ellipses

before and after rush of syllables
and citation of footnotes

in puddles of ripples
adding petrichor to the score

like ethereal fluid of gods
poured out to tease devotees.

war reads like a poem
Keketso Adorn Mashigo

for palestine, we raise the flag with you!

war reads like a poem, if you don't believe,
let me take you into the war story,
shut your mental eyes,
and open your imagination; now let's flow deep into the trenches.
in your imagination, picture this:
idf soldiers yank a palestinian girl by the hands,
while she yells for her mother whose israeli soldiers take turns
in digging her cunt with their hard-rock penises,
and bludgeon her in the face with the barrel of their guns,
the father looks through broken windows of his bombed house
as the other soldiers turn her only daughter into dog and rape her,
while he grunts and yells for the soldiers to stop,

his consciousness is snubbed by yet another mortar bomb which
pierce the remains of his house and cut both his legs hands and legs,
he cheats death, survives to tell the untold story of palestine,
or to spread fear, to tell of the horrors he saw.

the survivors of war with blood on their hands,
write their stories like scrolls in the hearts of their ancestors,
because blood means land, blood means freedom,
 it means war for independence,
they shape their tears into war,
use their voice to shoot like a government sniper,
because: it's an eye for an eye, lips are forever talking,
we are tired of bullshit, south africa is the blueprint to your freedom

in another same story:

imagine a ten year-old palestinian girl,
with bleeding lips, and broken fingers from scratching for water,
so her little sister can drink to see another day,
because israel denies them to drink from the rivers
their forefathers used to sit and wash the blood of their sins,
the sins of being born palestinian in country that hate them.

burnt olive trees, now the only food they eat are israeli lies,
imaginations filled with the screams of their dying folks.

her panties crusted with unwashed menstrual blood,
thick blood of a little girl forced into a woman,
her soul paralysed with fear, her filled with stories of terror,

just so she can give birth to puppets pumped with extreme fear,
no water to wash the shame of rape off her face,
or the dishonour of being defeated while still living,
her village is ransacked,
her god profaned by raping little girls and killing innocent women,
reducing them to things lesser than nothing,

can you picture that?
war is a poem written without soldiers.

when home is the only place
Keketso Adorn Mashigo

for palestine, we shall overcome!

when there is nowhere to run to but home,
we buy guns and guide the ships back to our home,
flow with the ocean back to the bones of our people,
fly like a tinge of brown dust,
back to home, where, like dust,
we will colour our land with the blood of our sword,
will write our names in the chest of the enemy,
restore history with the tip of our sword,
drip drip drip blood drops 'till it erases the ink of malice,
bang bang bang 'till our tears drips
and covers the face of the corpse of the enemy,
fight 'till history re-write itself,
we will never fear to offer our throats for our land,
to protect the dignity of our people,
because home is where the heart is,
where our umbilical cords were buried,
were the roots of our people origin,
home speaks to us in the language we suckled from our mothers' breasts,
because our mothers drank from the river that shaped our us,
rivers that made the structure of our bones,
rivers that gave us the shape of our language,
they picked from the garden full of birds,
a garden that gave them the sound of our language,
the river that made us who we are:
from the shape of our nose to the texture of our hairs,
our feet now yearns to kiss the grain of the sweets sand of our land,
our tongues yearns to speak the language of its mother,
to speak to the rivers, the mountains, the trees and birds,
to return is the right and virtue we grant ourselves.

when home is the only place,

the heart knows no other but the smell of home,
the eyes see but the beauty of home,
the legs walk but the walk is forever if we aren't going home—
carry your guns, carry the scars of your past,
the yells of your mother as she was ripped by a shell,
the thick black smoke of the night your home was bombed,
the yells of kids running for cover, the squeals of your mother
pleading to god to protect her kids while a bomb take her into pieces,
the shoes, toys and clothes of your baby soaked in blood,
the pieces of flesh israel said belonged to your father,
go home, *bang bang bang* shoot them all,
don't negotiate, you have run out of talking points,
the plot is already out,
the enemy is prepared to shed blood send you to hell,,
and drive you out of the land of your forefathers,
be prepared:
      guns,
     bombs,
    corpses,
   explosives,
  assassinations,
  imprisonment,
torture,
rape,
murder,
are part of the game—
to run away from home is a misnomer,
because you carry palestine in your soul,
there is palestine in your mind,
in your heart,
in your soul,
in your spirit,
in your blood,
screaming to be freed,
you can't run away from her screams,
her silent whispers for help are like a soul-sucking death,
the more you run, the more the whispers gnaw at you.

the silence that nip the good bud
Keketso Adorn Mashigo

i take a walk to the bush to smoke a blunt,
ask myself will god ever forgive us for our silence,
a nation scarred by the same bullet killing in palestine;
a young boy sits under the rubbles of
his mother's ransacked house,
smoke narcotics to drown
the traumatic sound of exploding shells in his head,
trying to reach for his late mother
who lives in the hell of his imagination,
imagination cursed by many years of loss and explosives —

the spell of our silence is spelled with
the name of dead palestinians on it,
with the smelling ashes of burning babies in palestine,
it is spelled on a clean white canvas,
with the blood of every palestinian dying every day,
the spell of our ignorance spells
the truth that can spell the jews regime into a reviewed system,
a project of a past they brought to offend the present,
to silence the present,
to rape the present and disqualify the present,
because every history *extremised* is a myth,
because every scar polished with the blood of
the other becomes a badge of deception,
at conception, they say, the ideology was a yearning,
before it yearned for blood,
relocated them from their land like a flood,
killing them and pretend it's a lie,
buy the revolution, televise it, shackle the propaganda,
the scenario is cooked by
a scenarist to boggle the brains that's the agenda,
it's palestine on the screenplay the victims are the innocent.

to the fighter.
cock your glock wear bulletproof vest spill 'em brains,
swing your knife at his fucking throat,
never let them capture you into the dark cells,
drop 'em bullets like they drop 'em shells from the sky,
live like every day is your last,
wear your pride like the scars of your mothers,
the ones you carried on the streets with brains hanging,
white t-shirts drabbed in a cloth of red crusted gore,
the little girls raped and dumped like rats to rot,
never let 'em apologise 'fore they knew
they were wrong when they shot your kind dead,
if israel has a right to defend itself,
palestine has a right to kill,
pump your nines with some bullets pack your words
sing your poetry,
yodel your names scream death before desecration,
ain't no crooked ideology can stand the test of creation,
even the gifted in wisdom can be fools sometimes.

to catch an oyster
Archie Swanson

deception is the key
daily wade the line of foam
and sift through fleshy offerings that tumble in
as if a clam-shelled prize
is furthest from your mind
avoid the rocky pools where oysters make their home
for they are watchful of your gait
and understand the danger of your beak

if needs be wait a day
a month
a week
until the moon is full and round
then with cover of falling gloam
stalk along the beach alone at lowest tide
tiptoe onto the weathered rocks
that hide the clearest pools

be careful not to show yourself above the jagged edge
wait your turn…
that moment when the oyster opens wide to dine
to filter flotsam from the brine
and surge of sea drains out again
leaving your victim high and dry
then without warning jam your bill inside
and pluck the tasty morsel from within

sangoma
Archie Swanson

sangoma is singing to the sea
shells around her ankles
bright bead-bracelets on her arms
she dances a sea dance
chanting her plaintful song
to a father gone

sangoma is dancing in the water
waves surge about her feet
wash through shells
her body sways
as she sings her song…
his lullaby

sangoma is chanting to the sea
arms flailing
her dress is green
the green of the land
her dress has patterned edges
and in the centre - a large red disc rising

sangoma has come to this sea
to this horizon
to these hills
below the dunes
where oyster catchers troll the shore
and wheeling shimmers of terns scatter by

Note: A Sangoma is a traditional South African healer

finding Sugar Man
Archie Swanson

In memory of Sixto Rodriguez – 1942 to 2023

on his 2004 Garden Route tour
I saw Rodriguez live
in a barn on a farm in Hoekwil
sucking a doobie and swigging Jack
singing well-worn vinyl tracks
in his nasal Detroit twang

songs that lit our teenage pathways
back in 1970
poetic lyrics and uncluttered tunes
wisdom from a Mexican American
dividing night like Slangkop light
sweeping over Long Beach dunes

where we camped out under milkwoods
waves whip-cracking on the shore
jammed on bongos and guitars
sang our Sexto choruses
under a display of stars
till first light announced the day

belted out back-cover lines
words resounding with our times
North Star beacon to our plans
fifty years ago
"… Sugar man you are the answer that makes our questions disappear…
For a blue coin won't you bring back all those colours to my dreams…" *

* From 'Sugar Man' on the Cold Fact album by Rodriguez.

WALL.
Abdullatif Khalid

Water, air, light, and land,
Elements that shape our world so grand,
Like a band.
Waves that crash, currents that flow,
Water sustains life, a force to know,
Like a snow.

Air that we breathe, unseen and clear,
A vital source for all to hear.
It carries whispers, songs, and cries,
And dances with the birds in the skies,
That appear in series.

Light that shines, a glowing sight,
From sunrise dawn to sunset night.
It warms the earth and gives us sight,
Guiding us through life with its bright light.

Land that we stand on, a steady base,
A home for all, a sacred space,
Not a race,
From mountains tall to oceans wide,
Land provides a place for us to abide,
To ride.

Water, air, light, and land,
A wall of elements so grand.
Together they create the world we see,
And give us life, endlessly.

PSYCHE IS NATURAL.
Abdullatif Khalid

Psyche!
I may underrate you but you still remain great
For you fear no threat
In the world so neat!
I call you human mind as the central force in thought,
That ought
The emotion and behavior of an individual!
Is it enough to romanticize about you?
Not all! Certainly not!
You are not called for from external being!

Psyche, oh wondrous maiden fair,
Born of earth and gentle air,
Intricacies of the mind,
Of nature's beauty intertwined.

Her thoughts like streams that flow and dance,
A rhythm set by natural chance,
With every breeze, her mind takes flight,
To lands unknown, beyond the sight.

She feels the sun upon her face,
And marvels at its golden grace,
As flowers bloom and birds take wing,
She sees the beauty in everything.

With every step, she feels the earth,
Her heart attuned to nature's worth,
And in her soul, she knows it true,
That all of nature speaks anew.

Oh, Psyche, born of earth and sky,
In you, we see our spirits fly,
For in your heart, we find our own,

And in your eyes, we feel at home.

THE TRUE REASON.
Abdullatif Khalid

We are the ones who don't believe
In a deity above or beneath
Our faith lies in reason and science
Not in a book or divine reliance

We find wonder in the natural world
And its complexities unfurled
From the smallest atom to the largest star
We see beauty without a need for a czar

We don't need a heaven or hell
To do good or avoid being fell
Our morals come from empathy and reason
Not from fear of divine treason

We may not have a god to pray
But we have each other every day
To share love, kindness, and compassion
And make the world a better place in action

So let us live with purpose and meaning
In a world without divine intervening
For we are the ones who take responsibility
And shape our own destiny with agility.

THE OTHER SIDE OF TOWN
Ojonugwa John Attah

There are days you sit down and think about the day you will pass;
What day of the week would it be, Monday, Tuesday, Sunday?
Will there be loud wailings or some sort of celebration?
A loud wail may be because people will miss you;
Maybe it could also mean that you owed some people money and they didn't take it before you left
A celebration could be that of a life well-lived or maybe one to make merry because you are no more
You can only see all these things from behind the curtain blinds – your position has changed to a different one – you lived yesterday but today, you are dead.
What will be in the minds of your parents, siblings, and friends?
They will cry – of course, they ought to – who will take them seriously if they do not shed a few hot tears?
But you know they will be others who will be happy, eh?
They will be in their best costume and come to witness in flesh and blood the reality of your departure.
They will fake the sympathy and the tears and dance in their hearts.
They will even ask for more plates of rice and goat meat and open bottles of Heineken with their yellow teeth.
They will pretend to mourn you a bit and sip from the cold bottle to calm them down.
You will see Caleb just looking into the distance – you owed him money but you know he cannot easily tell your family to pay him now since they will tag him "selfish."
You know you didn't want this, right?
Of course it is not your fault in any way – life, like they say, happens to all of us.
The way it hits us is all different and we remember life with different emotions and body language.
We do not choose our parts in this play – the director makes the rules.

I HAVE LOST MY FREEDOM
Ojonugwa John Attah

I have lost my freedom
It was right here yesterday where I left it
But I cannot find it today
Someone has taken it and doesn't want to give it back.

I have lost my freedom
Yesterday, I could walk freely to the places I wanted;
I could let the sun kiss my skin;
I could take in the smell of flowers and trees;
I could eat what I wanted;
But today I cannot find my freedom.

I have lost my freedom
My voice has been barricaded by weapons;
My hands have become numb;
My legs too weak to run a mile;
I swear I thought it was a joke!
Today I cannot find my freedom.

I have lost my freedom
Where will I find it today?
Who will tell me where they saw it last?
Will they recognize it from the photo I carry around?
Will they direct me to a place where it is sitting, waiting for me to take it home?
Where is my freedom?
It was right here yesterday. But it is nowhere to be found today.

WHEN HOME CALLS, YOU SHOULD ANSWER
Ojonugwa John Attah

What do you do first when you come home?
Who do you wish to see first?

When the rains have beaten you,
When the sun has smitten your soft skin,
When your hands have become calloused from working at the mines,
When your tongue has forgotten what the different tastes are,
When your nose dribbles your brain and falsely tells it what it smells,
When your shoulders are weighed down with multiple crosses that you bear,
When your mind is now filled with philosophies and one-liners, When your hair is full and needs to be trimmed at Abu's place,
When your heart becomes fragile from being broken over and over again by City girls,
When your idea of hope is a hand filled with sand, blown away by a rushing wind,

There is only one place that takes you back to restore to you everything you lost.

Would you turn the road before it becomes dark?
Would you leave the stories behind and create new legends?
Would you be happy to see Aisha, Farida, and Ummi?
Would the years away make you refuse to drink gin and play ayo with the men under the baobab tree?

The place that holds your umbilical cord is the same place that makes you welcome even when you don't recognize yourself in the mirror.
It calls you repeatedly so that you don't suffer many things that are unspeakable.

When home calls, you should answer.

My Father
William Khalipwina Mpina

I
Everyone knows my father was an alcoholic,
But on his funeral the pastor said his soul
Was destined to great things, and that his life
Was not a waste. I try to believe him,
But it's hard to see it that way.

I remember the nights he would come home drunk,
And the fights he would start with my mother.
I remember the times he would disappear
For days on end, and we would have no idea
Where he was or if he was coming back.

I remember the shame I felt when he would
Show up at school drunk, or when he would
Pass out by the road and I would have to
Carry him up in a wheelbarrow.

But I also remember the good times we had.
I remember the times he would take me to Mr. Muwawa's shop,
Or the times he would make me listen to MBC six o'clock news bulletin.
I remember the times he would make me laugh,
And the times he would tell me that I could do anything
I set my mind to or be like his elder brother, not him.

I don't know what the future holds, but I
Choose to believe that my father's soul
Is destined for great things. I choose to believe
That he is finally at peace, and that he
Is no longer in pain.

I choose to believe that his life was not a waste,
But that it was a journey that led him
To a better place. I choose to believe

That he is watching over me, and that he
Is proud of the person I have become.

II
For the love of my Father
A sincere response by Cousin Bubile Nyangulu Kayuni

Mhuuu! You have made me shed a tear
I remember how funny he was
I remember how good he was to us
Whenever he was sober
I remember the bad blood that was
There with his sister because of the nasty insults
He used to hurl at her

Yes, I remember how he fell so ill
And how I will do those trips alone to visit him
I remember how as young as I was
I sat my mother down one day to ask her
To forgive him and go and see him
For after all he was his blood brother
I remember the tears my mum shed
When she told me, 'I love him but it hurts?'

And oooh! I remember the sad
And solemn faces at his funeral
Anganga crying for his favourite side!
The wails from Aunt Stella, Aunt Hilda and Big Mama
Crying for the soul of their brother!

Malume Raza had his demons
But Malume Raza was a good man!
Hugs, William!

I Still Remember
William Khalipwina Mpina

I still remember the taste
Of the fruit you gave me,
Sweet and tart and juicy,
A taste of love in a sea of desperation.

We sat on the porch,
The sun beating down on our backs,
And you told me tales
Of your travels to *Egoli,* a land of gold and beauty.
I listened with wide eyes,
Enraptured by your stories,
Of the spirits, *mizimu,* you saw,
And the failed marriages you had.
I felt so lucky to be there, with you,
Sharing your stories and your fruit.
Those were some of the best days of my life, And
I'll never forget them.
Thank you, thank you
For the gourds of *masese* we shared,
And for the memories.
I hope you're still telling stories,
And sharing fruit,
With someone else,
Somewhere else.

My Mother Suffered
William Khalipwina Mpina

The shadow in her eyes
Was a secret she hid.
She toiled to raise a home,
But her heart was not at peace.

She stitched and sewed my clothes,
But they were never fine enough.
She filled my days with beauty,
But I could not see it.

She moulded me with gentle hands,
But I was too weak to stand.
She carved my soul with loving care,
But I was too blind to see.

She made me laugh when I was sad,
But her stories were not true.
She told me tales of faraway lands,
But I knew they were not real.

She opened up the world of books,
But I could not read them.
She was a true artist,
But her masterpiece was not me.

Now she is gone, and I am alone.
I will never forget her love,
But I will never understand her pain.

The shadow in her eyes
Is a mystery to me.
But I know that she was a builder, A
tailor, a painter, a potter,
A sculptor, a comedian,

A storyteller, and a librarian.

She was all these things and more.
She was my everything.
And now she is gone, but I will never forget
The love she gave me and the sacrifices she made.
She was a true artist,
And her masterpiece was me.

gurkha
Goodenough Mashego

(for legionnaires)

we send boys to war
they return as men
broken like ceramics
or never come back
some become prisoners of war
to opioids
existing in cages the size of their domes
never to find their way home
even after doors are flung open
they live not in physical addresses
but mental institutions
swelling the ranks of an invisible army
rebels without a cause
armed with weapons more lethal than guns
- schizophrenia
- delusions of grandeur
- paranoia
- entitlement

and
- hatred

they detest the system
which like termites nibbled at their youth
like maggots feasting on a cadaver
corroded their sense of being
collapsed them
and demanded they return as pimpled boys it marched off to war
to kill in yonder lands
to kill in the name of country
for a crown worn by one head
their hands glisten
with innocent blood spilled

in defence of a monarch they detest
we send our boys to battle
and wonder why they return bruised
their scars
permanent like tats
containing names of peers they buried
faces they see when sleep eludes 'em
memories summoned to soothe their survivor's guilt
peers accompanied by 21 dummy shells
and an opioid pandemic we mask
like we did an airborne bug
and do our true intentions

39 & 41
Goodenough Mashego

(for lesego motsepe and komla dumor)

our candles get snuffed 'fore they shed light to the world
consumed by ailments in rituals to appease no deities
we drop not batons they get snatched 'fore we relay to the next
my generation eclipsed by sadness our winter comes after spring
life no longer begins at forty: forty's the finishing line
we licking lips we jealous madiba had his victory lap
when lesego's star fades & komla departs in haste
my generation's here wondering if tomorrow is coming
we mourn souls swallowed by forces bigger than our resolve
pouring holy water we nazirites we touch no ale
our *au reviors* to our comrades resemble voodoo libations
yell 'fare thee well' pens on pads we scribble poems for ya
what do we say to a religious family with fresh tears on its cheeks
how do I tell parents whose daughter left not to fear the end
should we fear the end?
you shining lights like comets like tracer bullets we watch ya
huh!

erasure
Goodenough Mashego

they leave as boys
optimistic, pimpled and full of hubris
they return as men
cynical, scarred and afraid of sacrifice
men broken
into millions of pieces shrinks struggle to reassemble
traumatised men
scared of their own shadows they escape to opiates
men who have killed
often not in self-defense
their hands glisten with innocent blood
of women and children they killed
because politicians marked them for death
that's what broke these young men
who lost their boyhood
on a battlefield

Adventure
Martin Chrispine Juwa

Like leaves in winter, mocking birds sway,
sailing the sea of air, admiring clouds
but afraid of getting scorched while in flight,
for they think the sun is a tyrant.

Mice burrow underground, sniffing dust,
burrowing on, burrowing still, burrowing through
and passing by tree roots that open their deep eyes in awe
to admire their foraging associates.
They wish to see the underworld too,
but fear getting trampled upon by bulldozers.

In the rising of day
a dripping is weighty on the green carpet, but
the sun comes hiking slowly from the east,
weighed down by a load of flaming logs, and
dining on the morning dews slapping leaf surfaces.
The sun spreads his talons and tightly clutch
the unsuspecting fellows by the throat
and throw them onto the wings of the passing breeze.

Life in the smartphone age
Martin Chrispine Juwa

My life is an ancient scroll
rolled up open in this present time and space:
these intangible pieces of my journey are loud in there.
As seasons are birthed, flourish, and die slowly
like a wisp of smoke from camp fire,
my eyes are burning gems of questions without answers:
what is life? Most times I only think about sad June stars -
tender to the passing of months in this unseen cage
called life. Some days when the wind sighs through my window
sill, I think about the ghosts of these buried years and
our drowned friendships - bathing in Smartphones and Zoom,
such unfriendly loosening of love and care between us.
Though these days last long and their thorns are sharp,
life is a resilient time-eater, belted with steel shields...

Wishes
Martin Chrispine Juwa

I wish I had wings for flying.
I would float the atmosphere proudly,
hug and kiss clouds in my rotations.
I wish I had claws.
I would stick them in the belly of the sun
to enjoy his grumbling, if at all he goes upset
at people playing with his temper.
I wish I were immortal like Zeus
I would close my eyelids for a decade just for fun,
or crowd my memory with centuries of histories.
If I were a star, I would stoop down low to the earth, and
rent out my light to broken-hearted lovers, to
illuminate their sorrow, just for fun.
I have wishes, indeed, but I think being a man is
a blessing to cherish.
Just like the wind, a man can catch dreams
Even wishes cannot reach…

BABA VAENDA
Andrey B. Matambo

The first when home I got
To hug me on the veranda,
Mai Sandile was on point like a dot.
She said, "*Wawana baba vaenda.*"

My heart torn apart.
Again I came late.
Heavy the silence on the house
Like Ebola swept through twice.

Commando down,
Your sun now won't dawn.
Blood stained stanzas and verses.
This time I won't make fake promises.

I told you before,
Remember my letter?
If I had another dice to roll,
I'd pick the same father.

Christmas presents under the bed,
"Father Xmas passed through." you said
At night while we were asleep.
Memories still run too deep.

The holidays in Chongwe,
The grass greener;
The vacations in Mumbwa
With Auntie Anna…

Your insistence that I read,
Sweet storms when I failed.
You should give me strength father,
To climb to the top of the academic ladder!

When you went veggie
I stopped eating meat;
My solitude got big.
In few words we meet.

May my words not be blocked by any brick walls.
Papa, you are the best dad that there ever was!
I pray for your boundless bliss;
Please, rest in perfect peace.

Farewell, goodbye, adieu.
I swear I will miss you.
My god, my father;
My pen can't bleed further.

The first when home I got
To hug me on the veranda,
Mai Sandile was on point like a dot.
She said, "*Wawana baba vaenda.*"

(To the memory of Peter David Matambo: 21st June, 1964 -08 December, 2017)

DESPERATION
Andrey B. Matambo

You never speak your mind because you are
Afraid they may upset your source of bread and
butter, You obey even when it's not right,
You smile even when you're very hurt,
In bed at night you feel like a footnote
Because you always do when you should not.
The face in the mirror in anguish calls unto me -
"*Mambo*, when are we ever going to be free?"

THE A.I COUP
Andrey B. Matambo

We used to sit around an evening fire, trading stories
We used to lie lazy by the lake, I wrote you poems;
We used to turn off all the lights to watch movies like Troy
We flipped that room into one big cinema, didn't we? Oh boy.
I was in Lusaka looking for bread, you remained home in Accra.
You video-called me for hours over the recipe for cooking okra
For though we were many multiverses apart
When you sought solutions my face flashed first in your head.
Today you discard me in the same box you toss your forgotten stuffs
'Cause now you can have the world in your palms just by a few sounds or taps.
Ouch! Will we ever have another Will to fix it all when it all goes wrong?
Will this your new-found lover love you as deep as I used to, or as long?
Tonight I leave you in the hands of A.I!
My childhood sweetheart, goodbye.

Sex and Poetry
Edward Dzonze

A spliff of skunk
to ignite the night alive,
A Castle quart
to drown the conscience in stupor
I have a bar in mind
Where wisdom is served on papyrus tabloids
Behind the bar
Stands a lady all eyes on the dollars in my wallet
Puff, puff, puff
and do remember to pass on the spliff

Clothes on the floor,
She opened more than just a door
Between the two 'shits' of booze and smoke
She gave me her strawberry lips to savour
And together we wrote a verse
For dear reader to kiss and caress
Somebody getting laid between the lines,
Nobody is getting paid here
She licks at every drop of ink
Oozing from my writing pen

She loves the country style-
I have a hot sausage to deliver
Before the night gets cold in her mind
A sumptuous breast to fondle
In rhymes and rhythmic currency
Two curvy hips to detour the mind towards lust
Crying and moaning as she do-
all the music desired to turn the mattresses into a soulfully
frenzy One more round of the whatever
Before she forgets where my pen is
Maslay Queen manyama
Pabraai stand varikutsvira yekukara nyama

Waiting for the Rain
Edward Dzonze

Dirty dishes to clean
Before a meal is served-
A metaphor to what the country have been,
Mungoshi's little tin toys is all irony to the system undefined
The long wait awaits a little waiting
The Old Man strums the old tune
All lost to the taste of days

A bone is cast, to feed the hungry
We nod, clap and dance in our silence
The hype of it all is our resilience
The song taught us thus-
To throw away the dishes
And hold tight to a dirty mind
The ballot is soon gone
Before the mangy dogs bow for a bite

A new sun
beckons for Lucifer,
The setting looms behind
There is plenty of sugar for blind Mandisa beyond Manyene
The dusty streets awaits a pour
To dispel the stink of sewerage from its caption
Beneath the thought of waiting,
Hope is the grime on the dishes
Whatever the Chef cooks,
The waiter serves us everyone's wishes
Crucified on the same cross
Where an official oath awaits resurrection

Garabha awaits a different reign
The people awaits his churn
We nod, clap and dance through our actions
Pretty Betty is tired of counting the stars alone

She awaits a drop to dowse the flame in her pants
The long wait awaits a little more waiting
The dirty dishes we threw away
Cannot clean the dirty mind
The Dark Cloud above
Is no sign of a political reign

Wet dreams from the heavens

Edward Dzonze

The dry ground
Opens wide its thirsty arms
Pattering rain drops
Whispering wet dreams from the heavens above
Pretty clouds kissing the ground from the sky
When nature is the muse of seasons-
Sweet love is abound
Rainy days upon us, pretty clouds kissing the ground in a tranquil shower
Dry grass shedding dusty overalls from the kiss of pretty clouds
A life here birthed from this intercourse

IHEANYICHI
Chisimdi George

Great things has happened.
Celebration galore in fullest.
The ocean voices herald your birth.
Iheanyichi, the son of the soil.
On the top of the everest is the
joy of our ancestors.
Extinction was averted by your
birth and it is hope to our linage.
Iheanyichi!!.
Wailing weeping and worrying
are over.
The watchman has arrived.
Your coming to this family,
consolation and strength to the
elders.
Father priest prophets
and watchman to us.
Our passing is not in vain now.
The continuity of men of
thousand hands has reduced
with your birth Iheanyichi.
Iheanyichi!!
Rottenness has engulfed the land.
Looting enthroned and installed. .
Firewood as electricity.
kwashiorkor a regular visitor.
But your coming iheanyichi
the land has open up its incense
of calmness.
Our maidens now dance in hope.
For the elders, the sufferings are
over.
For me the father, there is a saviour
in my house.
Iheanyichi!!.

Your coming has increased my joy.
Together we will uphold our
culture.
Our festivities will not drown in
Niger again.
Our tongue will not try again to visit
the land of the spirit.
Our pride identity and unity is in
you iheanyichi!!.

COUPLING
Adiela Akoo

Tossing and turning, words won't let me sleep,
rhyming and coupling, emotions running deep!
I contemplate waking, to write it all down,
but don't want to disturb you, don't want you to frown!

I try very hard, to remember each word,
over and over, silently, unheard!
I plan by the morning, to record it afresh,
but duty takes precedence, so it remains just a wish!

When I finally find time, to ink it all in,
my mind has already, recycled the thing!
So I stare at the paper, trying hard to recall,
that great wonder, that would've impressed you all!

But the words refuse to come, like they did in my bed,
so it may very well be said, that my very best work, remained in my head!

(a contemporary sonnet)

as the rain pitter-pattered
Adiela Akoo

as the rain pitter-pattered on the roof
all else was quiet
except for a car going by in the distance
you don't like driving in this weather you said
I said I love standing in the rain –
that's when prayers are answered!

as the rain pitter-pattered on the roof
a search for the umbrella ensued
but it had already been taken
a reminder to be prompt – on both counts
you'll be waiting at two!

as the rain pitter-pattered on the roof
I gazed out the large glass windows
watched as the parched earth was quenched
appearing fresh, green, renewed!

and I pondered this curiously crazy life
and the things I failed to grasp as a girl
but thought I understood now as a softer, wiser
woman I thought about life and death…
I thought about tonight's dinner menu too…

as the rain pitter-pattered on the roof
in this quiet, leafy street
I didn't hear anything else, nobody did
as intruders slit the throat
of my friend across the street!

MILITOCRACY
Dickson Saba

In rural lands, suffering was profound,
A formidable government, in shadows it's found
With armed forces and militants all around
Iron-fisted rule, in fear we were bound

Freedom of speech, a deceptive guise
Yet freedom denied once voices did rise,
Constitution ignored, with laws they'd revise
To the detriment of masses, their demise

Gunfire echoed, the metallic stench of blood
Countless corpses, in the military's flood,
Who shall rescue us from this mournful crud?
Sacrifice for freedom, in tears, we've withstood.

The cry of the masses, a plea in the night,
We were saved from darkness, into the light
Democracy promised a future so bright
With smiles on faces, once hidden from sight

Freedom, the anthem, our hearts did elate
The flag of peace, we celebrated our fate,
But democracy crumbled, we couldn't negate
Corruption's corrosive, a cruel twist of fate.

Corruption, the root, all evil sowed,
Into the government, like a virus, it flowed
Worse than the military rule, our nation erode,
Tribal conflicts, despair, nepotism's ode.

Democracy's promise, a dream we did chase,
But it allow power to consolidate,
Wealth circled the elite, in this endless race, Now,
for military rule, we yearn, a drastic embrace

WHAT A COLD WORLD
Dickson Saba

In the frosty breath of a world grown cold,
Beneath the starless canvas of night's grand
design The moon, a fading ember, slips away,
Into the dark abyss, a fate malign

Cold breeze, cold world, in eerie accord,
The trees waltz to its chilling call,
The resilient thread through adversity's grasp, Yet
the frail hearts, they falter and fall

In frigid realm, masses indifferent,
Like serpents, they consume without remorse,
Devouring riches, heedless of the need,
Leaving barren trails along their course.

Cold breeze, cold world, a relentless foe.
It claims the mightiest, the warrior's soul Eroding
roots deep within like cankerworm's toll, A hero's
great fall, a sorrowful toll

The feeble bear the brunt, the strong find joy, Yet
the cold breeze and world's unyielding snare
None escape their grasp, a relentless ploy, Destiny
weaves our stories, with tender care.

CELESTIAL REFLECTION
Dickson Saba

Illuminating moon
Blindfolding sun
Attractive stars

Radiant sun
In all it's power
Still stoops low
For the moon to give light

Like sun
With a strong light
Even after been famous
They crave in people
To be like them

The moon cool and milky white Has the sum, hot and blindfolding With its power
Behind to suite through Illumination that distinguishes

They inspire people
To aspire greater thing
Before they expire
Just as they have always been

The stars
Far and tiny in the skies
Embedded is an expensive beauty
With great admiration and attraction

They are radiant
Although might be far
But they are attractive and fascinating

what 'll they be seeing?
Chenjerai Mhondera

i don't like the way women look at me,
in winter,
or at some function, in summer
in the city

especially in my short hair,
and unfettered complexion.

they make me feel the
power of their lust,
dragging me, all the way,
off my comfort,
off my confidence
to where their lust, last.

calling

Chenjerai Mhondera

make me
smile, laugh, love,
awww, relaxed, drool,
wow, nerd, think,
strong, confused, afraid,
sad, cry, sob and angry

because, i miss the touch
and feel of them all -

everywhere, all over me

IT WILL BE OKAY
Antreka Tladi

In the silence of the winter night
I tug myself into cold sheets,
Into a bed furnished with grief -
Tears spilling on the pillows.

I sleep on with a wearied heart
Curled up like an Okapi knife -
Beside me; an empty space,
A body's outline of a loved one.

There are no more cosy night talks
To cut the silence of the cold night,
Then I would open my heart's door
Like a shed of tools or words;

Looking for something like "sorry"
Or "it will be okay", but my thoughts uncinch
Like an old family photo album,
Memories nudging me to smile again.

A BRIGHT FACE, A GUIDING LIGHT
Antreka Tladi

Have you seen her face
Appear in the sky,
Saw it fade and erode away
And you wanted to cry?

Then a handkerchief offered
By a hand, trembling –
The world all dark
The sun behind clouds, waiting.

Everything rise;
Your emotions, your tears,
A body from a chair- the rain rise
Upward, and summer comes from below.

The sky return itself to blue
Your grandmother's face reveal its rays
From behind the clouds
As the sun in your troubled days.

You see her face clear and bright
As she had always been;
Caring and compassionate,
Always your guiding light.

The Stench
Jabulani Mzinyathi

The acrid rotting carcass
Vultures now airborne
Descending in hundreds
Hyenas biting off chunks
Green bottle flies singing
Singing nauseating songs
Thick hairy maggots writhing

The moral compass long lost
The putrid ways found justification
The ravenous ways long took root
Villains attain warped sainthood
Shady characters turned celebrities
The stench of it nauseates our people

On The Prowl
Jabulani Mzinyathi

The grotesque primeval beast
Gnarled and knotted silence
The village in a web of fear
The goring primeval beast
Rabidly biting all in sight
Striking terror as it gallops
This half man half beast
Villagers scurrying for cover
The primeval beast on the prowl
An insatiable appetite for flesh
Washing it down with sweat and tears

The Same Dog
Jabulani Mzinyathi

You get drunk on it
You stay inebriated
The addiction sets in

History is replete
Those lessons forgotten
Louis XVI under the guillotine
No lessons ever learnt

The likes of Benito Mussolini
That hail of bullets in Romania
Not a tear shed for Ceasescu
Target practice for troops

Ferdinand Marcos toppled
A lesson from the Phillipines
Samuel Kanyon Doe died
There on the streets of Liberia

Mengistu lives here today
A failure playing advisor
There is bitterness in that grave
The lesson will never take root

A Hooligan's Dark Paradise
Joseph Daniel Sukali

The breeze of dawn kisses his face aloof
As sun-rays peep through holes in the roof
The cock's crow is his alarm
He abandons his bug-infested paradise
In the bush behind the *gowero*, he answers the call of nature
Before you know it, he is in the tree that hid him
Devouring mangoes as flies sing praises in his face
Another day another trip through hell to paradise

The pigs chant his name in their hunger and anger
They get *vimbuza* energy to the shine of his yellow teeth
Even pigs can smell the odour of his Sunday-only bathed Lord's temple
Then the blatting begins in the goat house
As he opens to another barefoot chase
In his windowed shots, his buttocks smile as they wave goodbye at every step
Another day another trip through hell to paradise

The sun is ready to hug the west in its red face
Goat milk and tubers fixed his lunch before he left them
After mapping his body with water in the name of cleaning
He leaves for the supposed "elders" video show
14 summers old but his imagination already undresses every woman he sees
He walks home with his in-between twitching and leaking
As he enters his *gowero* ready to choke his beating heart until it vomits
The bed bugs smile to the death of the *Koloboi*'s soul
Another night in the Hooligan's dark paradise

Aborted at Birth
Joseph Daniel Sukali

I was three months old when my grandparents denied me
They did not wait to see me, they detested me while inside
I shed my first tear while still in my mother's womb
My father who had raped my mother was the first to run away
She never said it till I grew and the bump was no longer invisible
I was a mistake and a curse before I even got formed fully

Six months later I was Hope to my depressed mother
A strong 15-year-old girl disowned by her parents
I never blamed her any time she contemplated suicide
At times I felt like sleeping for life to give my mother peace
A miscarriage would be a relief than what I put her through
Guilty and depression slowed my growth and delayed my birth

Ten months now and I am still stuck to the umbilical cord
I have survived medical and stress-induced abortions
I still never understood why mum kept me when I was a burden
The world is a cruel place for a girl child I can sense it from here
I already know pain, and suffering flow in my bloodstream
Am scared of the outside but it's time I wake up from the dream

First breath old and mother walks away for life leaving me an orphan
My first deep life inhale and am already walking tall deep in hell
But I am not surprised by the abandonment, I am a fruit of rape
Forbidden from conception, her final slumber is proof that I am a curse
I was only forced on her but her love soldiered on to give me a chance
For her love, I hung myself with my umbilical code to slumber with her
Here I am with smiling tears looking at death in the eye, aborted at birth

Where Do We Go When We Sleep
Joseph Daniel Sukali

As the eyelids lose their erection, the door to the soul closes in consciousness
Consequently opening the gate in the realm of sub-consciousness
As the body shuts down and starts making love with inactivity
The fascinating duality of body and soul becomes a reality
As the mortal-self takes a test drive of death
The immortal goes on a witch-hunt for memories
While we close our eyes and shut our brains in sleep
We awake the monsters of the mind in dreams
The wars we have ignored and forcefully let go
Burn down the tranquillity of our souls in nightmares
Reality gets proven to be nothing, but a perception
What scares us in the dark is not darkness but mental pictures
The same beautiful flowers under the love of light
Turn into living shadows to the kiss of darkness
The same brain that dictates everything in consciousness
Turns into a slave bowing down to the instructions of the deeper self

As the eyes close, inner creeps the silence
Slowly floats the soul outside its body
There is death in sleep only with the heart still beating
The amount of nothingness is quite sound in snoring
Everything is put on pause as the body decays with rest
The senses are still sensible without you making sense of them
What sensible senselessness!
But where do we go in the blink of such a tranquillity?
How does the inner clock tick while the self is in limbo?
The time lost is just mortality brought near to it's grave
Every slumber party is rapport-building with the mother of slumbers
Every time we rest is a step towards resting in the peace of the soul
We're immortal heavenly beings playing humans on earth
Born only to have enough time to prepare for our own death
Our final breath is the rebirth of our immortality hibernated in humanity

We age as time passes just to get back to the roots of our pre-mortality
So if you ask me where we go when we sleep, I will tell you: Home
Sleep is just a train taking us to the other side in an indescribable form

Burnt Offerings
Kennix Odera

We held hands and enjoyed the rain
Ours took the form of a flower
It stayed soft and sweet
What a heaven in itself

Now it has charred
My bubbles are bursting right in front of me
I am haunted
By the genuine desires that compelled me to get attracted soon.

She has crucified me,
And lied that my patience bar is too high for others with faces like mine,
That she loves me,
I have continued waiting for her.

She demands for kisses and hot photos,
But she is always held up when it is my turn,
She shouts at me 'The city is full of relatives, we must keep this a secret!'
I have failed to fulfil a desire which I yearn.

My heart feels numb sometimes,
I look at my efforts and I can see the cracks,
It is going to end,
She has sent me back to my childhood bedroom,
The more I have loved her, the more she has disappeared.

After life
Kennix Odera

At his last sigh he said;

"My end has come,
To the mother of my children;

The vast sums,

To my son;

The family tree,

To my daughter;

The family pet,

To me;

A decked tomb"

HIS Majesty the QUEEN
Kennix Odera

The knots of uneven progress have been her story,
Today she is sitting at the table of men,
She is instructing stallions,
She is now happening,
She is the whole!

They are gazing at her stare,
They see that; this is the day she became strong enough,
She has built an army,
It is winning Kingdoms.

The world isn't so big,
She carries the crown on her head,
Everyone is admiring her steps,
They are narrow but wide,
The world doesn't know her like that,.

It is heyday,
She has become a gallery of royalty,
Her tongue is a sword,
That is what has brought her here,
She is now walking into this room; where she is the only one who looks like HER.

Her intentions have refused to be caged birds,
She can't stay at home when there is a war to be won,
And has instructed them to call her when they want something done,
She is not ashamed of her 'anger'
On this altar; she has strangled the power that prevents HER from being ALL.
The she-mountain is here!

Wakeful
Philip Miti

As the world is quiet
And snoring
I'm wide awake every
Night,

Every night I try to get
Myself to bed but
I fail,

For all the regrets comes
Rearward to me at night,
I can't sleep and Insomnia
Every day attacks me,

I'm scared, feeling much
More worse at night,
The night really scares me
Terribly,

At night demons come to
Me, I feel them, I see them,
I can't sleep even a bit,
I can't even close my eyes for
a second,

Each day when the day is
Ending
I'm in fear, I can't bear the
Night
And so weaker I'get, as time
Pass from day to night

Lullaby rhythms don't work
And so as sleeping pills,
The night scares me, killing
My sleeping rhymes

"I'm scared I can't sleep."
Wakeful I'm

She Melting Me To Love
Philip Miti

I never believed in love
At first sight,
After eyeing her from
A distant
    "I now believe".

I'm heisted into a love
Believer
She's a Professor, making
Me wonder if...
      "it's Love or money
Heist?"

Slowly, majestically
Cat walking
 In her faded yellow
Banana shoes.
    Sparkling her beauty
As Margot...
Just like Maru, Yellow is
Now my favorite color.

So distractive as a naked
Human being she is,
Making the other girl invisible
Before my naked sight.

I don't know her name, I
Wish to call her
    "Mine".
In my dreams giving her my
Heart as an organ donor,

She's so cute I must be

Dreaming,
Can someone pinch
Me back to life?

If being sexy was a crime
She should be guilty as
charged,

And if I kissed her, the heart
Of my passion,
Shall certainly melt her to love
With me.

Making me want to bounce
On you as a trampoline....

"For her beauty is "Magically
Melting me to love."

You're A True Friend Of Yourself
Philip Miti

You're the only true friend
Of all seasons
 You're yourself good friend
From birth to death,

Not even your birthday giver
Can ever fit to be your friend,
      "Nor in dreams,
    Perhaps your closest enemy
I guess
 "But not your true friend".

The only true and trusted friend should be no one
 "But you".

Is only you who knows the
Measurements of your
"Love,
And the *patientness* of
Your patience,

No one else but only you
Understand you, your
"Kindness".
The pinch of your laughter,
Concern and willingness.

What makes you happy or sad?
You know it better.
How to control you, limit your curiosity,

Only you can mix that
Happiness with faith
The only one who can spread the
Love, peace and unite it to you.

You're the best mirror of yourself
Either broken or not
You'll still see your reflection beautiful or not.

You're the first disappointment
Before anyone else of you,
You can see it coming or feel it
For it's coming from you.

You're nothing but your own true friend of all seasons…

The universe
Abigirl Phiri

As big as it is
It's not conducive for us all
Filled up with woes
Which many can't talk about
Yet existence is a must
Would you dare take your own life?
Or instead just go with the flow
Starring at the sky
Counting the stars
Living in the moment
Twiddling your fingers
Hopeful of change
Reminiscing
Of the good old days
And the next day to come
Striving to look for your talent
In a bid
To outdo your problems
As starry black as the night is
So are our dark sins

Ode to a pen
Abigirl Phiri

Without you, life would have been dreary
Our mental capacity and faculties
Would be forlornly lost without you
Although you hide in the shadows of cases
You are mightier than the sword
The scribes and pharaohs can attest
Nothing beats putting pen to paper
The liberating and exhilarating scribbling
experience So spell bounding like your indelible ink
Without you
Then our legacies are devoid of magnificence

Zim now
Abigirl Phiri

People are oblivious
Of the obvious things
We are struggling in silence
As we sing Silent Night
Calamities continue to burgeon us
Left, right and center
Uncertainty is a fore gone conclusion
Illustrious life and careers an illusion
Who is to blame?
Wearing badges of blamelessness
Maybe we are cursed?
Accursed of things we know not of
Yet we are just trying to make ends meet
As we meet and greet in the dirt streets
The hope is
We will come out of this joke unscathed

Beautiful
Adaobi Charlyn Chilekezi

But beauty is more than just my outward grace
It's the resilience etched on my face
For I've battled storms, walked paths unseen
Yet I wear a smile, radiating a queen

I am a winner!
Adaobi Charlyn Chilekezi

Deep within me burns a relentless fire
A hunger for triumph that will never die
I'm a winner, not by chance, but by choice
Through dedication, hard work, and a powerful voice
So, let the world witness my rise with glee
For I am a winner, and forever I'll be

Altered spirits
Adaobi Charlyn Chilekezi

In ancient times,
Before the predators came
Africa stood tall
With its vibrant flame

A land of secrets
A land of wisdom
Thriving in glory
Flourishing in pride

The beat of the djembe
The sound of the ekwe
Filling the night with
An enchanting display.

History has been lost
Africa has been altered
Trials and tribulations
But our spirits are unbroken.

Through oral traditions
History did unfold,
Preserving legends,
Preserving wisdom.

Like the starry night sky
Obinna Chilekezi

I am African
Skin black, like the feathers of crow
My lips brown, deep as the soul
Nose flat, breathe-full and beauty
Above all, I am African
Black, beautiful as a starry night sky

A change of taste
Obinna Chilekezi

This tongue ever used to the palm
Liquid fresh from the backyard tap, whitish
Bubbling in kindness, soothing
Good gift of our goddess Bacchus

Thought I have tasted it all
Till this Saturday, on my dining table
An O' Orla Maritima, Vinho tinto
 Portuguese tapped, 12.5% vol.
Instruction foreign
Proveniente de casta
De excelente sabor e bouquet
Not even a kind word in English

Carton wrapped
Colour red like blood
Taste good while chilled
Inviting, tongue twisting

Colour quite different
Even in taste from our whitish
More powerful than tapster's best
O' Orla, just inviting …

I have begun to fall
Asleep, even too soon …

Good
Obinna Chilekezi

Look good
Feel good
  A good world
    To be …
Good

Darling star!
Adebayo julius O

I am jealous of you—Darling star.

I am envious of your happy life,

Each time nightfall crawls over the sun,

And night had her reigns;

it's either the moon or you

but each moment;

you glow like a Diamond in the sky.

I wish I could pluck you,

my charming twinkle little star.

I think I will have you-

When the rain decline,

I will climb the tiny pole

to see your home,

if I couldn't; never you make a jest of me with laughter,

I promise to send you my soul-full of beautiful gist

When the time is ripe to send him on heaven's errand.

I wish I could pluck you
my shining twinkle little ✸
each time the night reigns.

Time flies!
Adebayo julius O

Time runs faster than a cheetah.

If you think is fast-

Prisoner will wrestle you.

If you think is slower-

Debtors will wrestle for being selfish.

Despite how debatable she was;

God made it to be equally shared.

The prisoner and the debtor could argue;

Prisoner: come sit here with me here,

And, see how much the sky keeps still,

How much the clock's hands move slower

Then;

The debtor—

Staring much at the calendar,

Felt the days ate the cheetah's feet.

Either right or wrong—both were,

For the past of the days

A man liveth,

He has two lessons and memories left behind.

Some days we remember our smiles,

Sometimes our tears,

Sometimes our treasures,

Sometimes our suffering,

Sometimes the times, the truthful lies,

Sometimes the truth our cowardice couldn't alter,

Sometimes the doubt we had in ourselves,

Sometimes the times we believed in each,

Sometimes the times we had a fight,

Each time we thought of the past,

Either on our:

Bed's of love,

Bed's of roses,

Bed's of stones,

Bed's of thoughts,

Bed's of sorrows,

Bed's of tears,

Bed's of regrets,

Bed's of appreciations;

The two lessons of memories

Will take her share—

The wrong memories or the tough ones

made us stronger, and we never wish it comes again.

The other memories—

Take her share,

Brought the glimpses and the things of the misses:

The days with love ones,

The days with family,

The day friend (s) left without a tell,

A day family left without a goodbye,

Then, we all agreed,

And, we wish:

We could draw the time backward,

We could ask God a chance-

To tell the sky to swim back forth.

What will be our excuses?

Some lives we couldn't live?

Some wrongs we could have put a right?

Some jokes we ought to have put laughter?

Some people we wouldn't have let go?

Some help we could have rendered?

Some hearts we could have healed?

Some forgiveness we could have to yield to?

Well, if you have a chance,

To play yours right,

do so. Time flies,

And each moment she flies,

It took the pictures of all the memories.

A PLACE CALLED HOME
Adebayo julius O

A place called home,

A hand called peace,

A thigh called pillow,

A leg called support,

The true African hood of loving you.

Wherever did I go,

Wherever I will be,

When ever-

what shall we eat and drink

took me out,

Do you ever think a man will forget home?

A place he feels welcomed?

A place he is treated like a king?

A place someone behind the closed door fights for him?

Look, Asake mi,   *(look, my darling Asake)*

Mosunmola mi,   *(my adorable joy)*

Omo Are kankanfo, *(the daughter of a Yoruba war lord)*

Idi aran ooo, *(beautiful lady)*

omo iya oyindamola, *(daughter of her mother)*

Egbon Agbeke mi, *(Agbeke's sister)*

Ti se aburo Moremi owon. *(Kid sister of Yoruba heroine-Moremi)*

The sacrificial's days will go unnoticed,

If your effort on me does not give birth to success.

Look, arewa eledumare, *(look, my God's angel)*

Won't you be ashamed?

If your effort and prayer didn't eventually birth us success.

Look, won't you be guilty?

If our children weren't raised on God's path.

Mo mope olorunsogo nbe, (I know there are richly made home)

Sugbon surulere ma n'uyi pupo. (but patience is virtue)

Look, instead of war;

Take me into your arms and fortify me.

Look, instead of confrontation;

Take me into your closet and talk to my heart.

Look, instead of picking the fight;

Pick up the prayer and talk to God on my mother's behalf.

Look, instead of nagging for the next meal;

What if you think of how we can make it possible.

Look, instead of putting the blame on me;

Why don't you think I am your responsibility-

a baby adult who needed a train.

Each time displeasure crowds your mind;

Each time the devil whispers to you

My wrong deeds;

Can you scold me with the right,

draws me nigh with the left,

like a mother does?

"Cos outta there are tempting;

Outta there are competitive;

Outta there are only for the strong;

Outta there are misleading tutorials;

Outta there is struggle for survival;

Ain't no peace outta there."

Guess what comes to my mind

Each time I thought of-

Going home,

running home,

fighting my way back home,

Knowing fully, I got a home in our home.

Where no one can hurt me,

Where no one can undermine me,

Where no one can take my pride,

Where no one can defeat me.

And, each time I am running;

Each time I turn away

from the struggles and the failures,

I am glad that you are my home,

And the building is our shelter.

In Africa:

The beautiful heart of a woman makes us a king;

The virtuousness of motherhood

makes them the kids' Lord and trusted ally;

Ain't tricking you,

Mother's days ain't about the beautiful lady out there,

But the woman who gives it all to raise us,

whom back I first had sweet dreams.

-A place called home!

PYRAYERS END HERE
Lucas Lungu Jr | HOLY POET

Tonight I can write about my mental health before I begin to masturbate.

I forget I'm a Muslim. I forget I'm a Christian—

though in one of my prayers have told God, "i left a bag of my things in your stomach."

to just say my mental health has been on life support.

Chapter one;

this person is surviving d e p r e s s i o n.

Chapter two;

Inside this poem my father is a little boy learning how to read

a Quran, a half poem and a boy on burning photographs—

Chapter six hundred and two;

I saw visions of broken boys on transit cameras,

posturing for grief to poke out their happiness,

Chapter three;
May we never forget how much i survived everything you labelled attention seeking!

GOD BLESS YOUR SINS
Lucas Lungu Jr | HOLY POET

Haven't depression watched me pray while God was busy drowning in my mouth,

And I looked like I was masturbating when i stood there—

while these ropes were saying Amen, Amen!

—You know who your mother is,

& I don't know mine, so I could not pray properly.

I tell you to hide my body where you put your faith,

when you come to pray to this mosque,

because I carved my depression in the size of your prayers,

but they did not reach heaven that Friday,

& rest in peace, rest in peace—

This is a worship hymn I wrote together with my elder brother who committed suicide yesterday.

In the name of God, you would say,

"At 19 you're just starting your life"

While these suicide ropes, pray in tongues,

—others partake holy communion to be forgiven their two sins, one for me and the other my brother,

Mum, I want you to know that, there's no "fake depressed"

Salaam—

MY COUNTRY
Salmista Cortês

It's still too early to talk
It's still too early to,
to blurt out
What I see a lot
What is every
I see.

Good and brave things
Sweet and bitter things
Blessing Nation
With double heart.

Here there are leafy cities
That should be more
cities
There are lakes that
turn into rivers
There is the dead of night and the
haunting day.

Everything is perfect
Joy here is hopeless
Happy nation with a welcome
unparalleled
Treat everyone well without
exception of racial color.

I don't regret this
nation
I will always sing the anthem of
your song
I will take the boat with you
her until she grows
Your deeds will generate a day
development.

Our cities will be
more cities
Our logos will be
fewer rivers
Our love will expand
to the ends
Our smile will find
comfort when
astonishment.

It will be more of us
We will be more nation
We will be the mouth
We will be the way of the heart
My country
My nation
My country
Forever, live, in my
deep heart.

I WISH IF I HAD WINGS
Salmista Cortês

If I had wings,
in the dead of night I would bring you
the scent of unforgettable dreams,
the best most beautiful flowers
of this universe.

If I had wings,
I wouldn't allow any cold
 torment your body,
If I had wings,
would take you to imaginable places,
would make you discover the seven planets, and
one more that I discovered a few days ago,
incidentally, the best of all.

I wish I had wings,
If I had wings,
would be your favorite transport,
your fanning in the heat,
would change the world of humans,
bringing good news to each continent,
a new reality of love.

Look, if I had wings,
I would fly every day
in your thoughts.
Oh, speechless!
Thinking...
As...
I wish it had wings.

THE BLACK CRY TO MOTHER AFRICA
Salmista Cortês

My lady Africa
With hard hair, with sharp braids
So golden and extremely tattered
 In a decent skirt, innocently raped
Of intelligence in averse, but all coveted.

With beautiful beauty, with dust on your face,
With tears from the past, present and an opposite future
Many men have enjoyed you
They laughed at you, but they did not take your virginity
That promiscuity is still observed
You can still see that defenselessness of authority.

Since ancient times
You made black people great individuals
 You took care of them as always, you tried hard to overcome the pain,
Instead of blood in a much worse adolescence phase
Mother Africa, you had to give birth to us
The heroes together with you bled, but still the abyss continues.

Your children are widespread
Your inheritances left were hidden blindfolded
They cannot be felt with the naked eye,
 Though abundantly seen
Please come and take refuge with us,
 as until now we have only eaten the leftovers.
My mother Africa, where are you?

Stops in a Winged Bracket
Okolo Chinua

(After visiting Borno)
Like a camel of solace I arrive this city to find that space is the beginning of everything here...
There are more grasses than people and a person found is a treasure sought,
At nights grasses come alive and a moving grass is not the wind in question,
To be here is to always observe the shadow
and absence requires flight..
In this city a person found is a treasure sought,
and space, is the beginning of everything...

Hands Sardined in Gold
Okolo Chinua

(After visiting Lagos)
A gateway into a myriad of bees is the first letter of this city...
Here, men are made of plastic and their wills of rubber..
Every morning an individual rises with the desire to be the sole needle that threads the seams of fortune,
The streets are jelly, little smooth but always packed,
And each voice towers above the other, a minstrel of babels...
In this city a pierced heart is uniform and people are bottles raining from the sky...

On The Journey of Returning
Okolo Chinua

(After visiting Rivers)
A solemn desire takes root and grows into a planted belief...
A sailor stands, winds grin, and home is just ahead..
In this river walk I have stood above water and have drowned,
I have swallowed and been swallowed..

The skies are cloudy and the grins become faces..
Maybe home is tomorrow away or farther,
Thanks to all that have been, I am nature and these walks bother me now not,
Perhaps I might thread, an oddysey riding arrows past hollows…
or maybe the beauty of a candle then as I melt, flames away from the sun…

The End of the Road
McLayode

[For Emmanuel Adefalu, an ambitious student of physics, who met his death in a moving coffin called car]

The saps of your bursting hope
Gelled with gestating mechanical mind
Would create an oasis in our disgusted desert
And for us pump an abundance

The vat of your fledging future
Wrapped up a springing depth of science wisdom
Would invent our dream rocket
And launch us to the space of carefree life

But on a day in a SAP contraption
A traveler must trash time and
Consign laws of motion to a heap of lies
And the spinning earth to a snail pace

Race on then traveler, destined
Just in time for the sapped shadows
Long, veil of a lurking crouching lions
Springing surprising sudden SAP traps
The road bi-forked, sudden, as in a dream
Vision blurred, the speeding human devised caved into
The blood dribbling paws of the lion

Scattered and shattered scrapes of broken glass
Vain shimmering shivers of contorted metals
In their millions of grosses
The contorted tortured you, prostrate on the tar
Mangled blood patterned
Another of our great sun
Plunged into an eclipse at noon

The Songs for and of a Benedict
McLayode

                              Son
                     Be blessed with a son
                     A stone thrown forward
                     Where you stop
                     Your son continue

           The wedding sounds tickle our ears again
        In vain do we keep the watch
        For you to call on us to yours

                    Your season of strident songs
For want of productive activities
You must sing stinging songs

           Each running year we must return
            To remind you of a runaway time
Faithful in being unfaithful
With your wilting virility

        Your taunting is not without significance
        But surely life is more than what you crave
        A great teacher once said
        Life is more than mating

        We know learned man of a religion
        Mixed with madness ruining its votaries
        Life is incomplete without a child in the living room
        Even if you achieve heaven and earth
The dying fire replaces self with ashes
The old plantain tree with a daughter sucker

            Your plantain dies to be replaced
And your fire cover its receding self with ashes

But certainly not in my own age
For the plantain cycle has changed
And there are fires without ashes
And should you leave me alone
I will gladly seize my hard earned rest

      Bang the door in our face learned man
      This time next season
      We shall call again and again
      Impotency is never known in our family
      Paternity dispels mouth left ajar
Like the bad door of an untenanted room

Strike the *agogo** harder
Let the metallic thing resonate
But reduce the hard beat on the drum
Great drummer lest the skin tears
Lest the skin tears…..
For we shall return again…
We shall….

*agogo – Yoruba word for metal gong

Tyrant Time
McLayode

Desertification of my dreams
......encroaching, insidious, on my fertile soil

Of my verdure of hope now
Stunned into imbecile silence

The Marvel of the Dandelion
Colleen Venter

Seed-laden parachutes, ready for take off
bursting forth in downy display
destined for the soil for regeneration
Almost see-through in its arrangement
Cotton-wool soft in a delicate sphere
Seed-laden parachutes, ready for take off
They unfurl from underneath
gathered, armed for their mission
destined for the soil for regeneration
Dandelions, having shed their petals,
prepared for their following cycle
Seed-laden parachutes, ready for take off
Patiently waiting for their cue
when the wind will set them free
destined for the soil for regeneration
A bountiful cushion of flimsy filaments
We admire their beauty in full array.
Seed-laden parachutes, ready for take off
destined for the soil for regeneration

I live in Fear
David Chasumba

I live in fear
Of crossing paths
With a dirty white cop
Of stop and search
Of stop and catch

I live in fear
Of saying wrong words
At the wrong time
To a wrong white cop

I live in fear
Of fleeing Dirty Harry
One of crazy white cops
When ordered to stop
Lest I get three pops
To the head, back or neck

I live in fear
Of resisting arrest by Dirty Harry
Lest I get tasered
Or worse, choked
With a knee in the neck
For nine minutes and 29 seconds.

I live in fear
Of standing in a parade,
Black man are the usual suspects,
Easy to single out one, in a charade

I live in fear
Of facing a white judge
Who knows all about black gangs;
The Bloods, The Crips,

And the chain gang

I live in fear
Of losing my mind
And sectioned in Bedlam
Where staff aren't so kind
To my kind, and mastered
The dark art of choking
Deranged Black men

I live in fear
Of going to my grave
Before I see a white cop
Pop an innocent white kid
In the head, neck or back

On Turning Fifty
David Chasumba

I saw liberation before a million years.
I saw black liberation dawn
On Rhodesia before Ian Smith's million years
And so, Black Bob was enthroned with cheers
In House of Stone
Then saw him dethroned with jeers
I saw how Berlin Wall fell
When winds of change raged
How rainbow dreams were uncaged
From goal of Apartheid hell
How Merry Michelle and Black Barry
Strolled into a White House
Built with slave blood, sweat and tears.

I recall my moment of joy
First time in bosom of a woman
My first-time pride and joy
Holding my black baby boy
My moment of grace
Sitting at the King's table
Like Mephibosheth dining on soy.

Now that I've turned fifty
I feel like Peter Pan, a kiddy,
I look down the road travelled
Grateful for the journey, the years,
The cheers, the tears, the fears,
The boy, the joy,
The life, the strife, the grace
And wisdom wrought in disgrace.
I gaze with anticipation
Down the road untravelled
Down the long road ungravelled.

The Daddy Issues
David Chasumba

How can I become a doting dad
When I was reared
By a protective hen
In a den without a dad

How can I lull my son
With a lullaby
When my dad loved beer
More than me, more than tea,
When every night
I lulled myself
To sleep with tears

How can I begin
To preach or teach
About fragility of life
When my dad died
In a car crush

How can I tell my daughter
Trust a man
Lust a man
When my dad fled our home
To a small house

How do I love my father
Who married my mother
But fell in love
With the liberation struggle

How can I forgive my dad
Who was a pub bird
But now frail as a leaf
A dry wind tossed leaf

I will become a doting dad
When I come to terms
With the deep pain
That lingers inside me
When I resolve the daddy issues;
The dad I had
The dad I wished I had
And the dad I wish to be

WEAVER BIRDS
Alfred S. Mukanaka

Weave me a home
Like day-old chicks, doves
Living together as one!

Weave me a home
Like the woodpecker
In a tree trunk, strong!

Weave me a home
Like the wagtail
Safe in someone's roof!

Weave me a home
Like the seagull
Flying above petty penguins!

Weave me a home
Like the high-flying eagle
Not a caged broiler chicken.

Weave me a home
Like a migratory bird
I can go and still come back.

Weave me a home
Like the homing pigeon
Not a mimicking parrot.

Weave me a home
Like the ostrich
So I can outlive the dodo.

Weave me a home
To move about like a peacock

Not a half-dressed turkey.

Weave me a home
To walk tall like a flamingo, crested crane
Not the wobbly duck.

Weave me a home
Like the grain eating guinea fowl
Not a scavenging crow, kite.

Weave me a home
Like the patient vulture
So I can wait for your promised feast!

Weave me a home
Not like the awful owl
But a tit, sunbird
To stand & sing proud & free!

Politicians are weaver birds
One tree, multiple nests!

THE MAGICIAN IN MY BED
Womba Nakazwe

Hush now hush now child Hush your pretty soul
For the magician lies in my bed
He disappears when you need him and when you want him he graces you with his shadow.
He appears when you least expect him, to hush your heart and soothe your soul.
He manages to calm the storm in you just so he can cause a hurricane.
He fixes you just so he can break you into a thousand pieces.
Hush now hush now child hush your pretty soul for the magician lays and lies in my bed
Every Friday night he goes into oblivion only to reappear on Monday like nothing happened.
 The magician in my bed sings songs of praise, smelling like a cheap motel he kisses me and I melt away into him I melt even though I taste the bitterness of her.
I weep as we swim deep into the ocean of his lies. The magician in my bed my savior and my destroyer.
An angel and a demon.
Hush now hush now child hush your pretty soul for the magician lies in my bed.
He sends flowers to mask the scents of his lies and chocolates to sweeten the bitter taste of his betrayal.
 He adorns me with all the shiny diamonds just so I can't see what he's doing in the dark, he numbs me with his caress and kisses just so I can't run from him
Hush now hush now child hush your pretty soul for the magician lies in my bed.

You Have Come Again
Wellington Nwogu

You have come again with your burgeoning belly
To munch our meat and to sap the succulence
Of our marrows; faithful eaters of our food,
And drinkers of our crude;

Tell us the taste of our mothers' food, you
Whose plates bear our rice and stew;
You steadily suck from our mothers' breasts,
Leaving no milk for the hungry owners; tell us the taste

Of our own mothers' breasts, you suckling adults of our
Mothers' nipples and eaters of another's bread and meat;
You steal our hopes in broad daylights, without gun,
Bullets or bow and arrows

You have come to guzzle up the waters of our rivers
And we repeatedly thirst in the midst of springing waters;
You bury your iron pipes in our homeland's womb,
You bury our dreams in your private pockets

Could you please tell us the colour of our crude
That which daily fill your faraway tank?
Your eyes like the eagles search out secrete
Things of our fathers' homeland

You have become the owner of another man's
Liquescent gold; who does not know that your
Steady light comes from the darkness of our birthplace,
And our pain: the mother of the gain that brightens up your hollow
face…

You have come again. You have come again with full bags
Of empty things; tankers of crude line our village
And township paths; and, we buy the fruits fetched from

Our own farms in dollars that we do not have!

BAD DEBTS
Kimutai Kemboi Allan

And tell the king loudly
Your kingdom will fall
A house of plastic cards
The rubble will be skeletons
Good and bad citizens extinguished
Democracy expunged from our dictionary
A book of bloodstained words
Orphans smiling at a tattered flag
Singing dirges for a national anthem
A state that swallows its people.
You have seen and heard the tale
A sun setting on your land
Apparitions of the dead yawning
Back to give you company
The owls of the night calling
Your name in the royal ceilings
A palace haunted by the past
Time to pay all the debts!

MASQUES OF DECEIT
Kimutai Kemboi Allan

Everyone thinks that I know. Writing
away at my desk, to appease my demons.
Pleasing the vigilant mind of a hawk-eyed
editor, oh they don't know! Behind my
rickety chair lies a pile, rejections!
I could sing them a few lines of my
song of sorrow, they believe I know. Like
I am a genius with words, the gods do
awe my concoctions. How can they say I
have the skill, I have eaten half my pencil.
And written just a few lines, my thoughts
have fleeted away. They lie in wait for
the book, to celebrate the art they
won't buy. And shout, "Our man is a
brilliant writer", my book is remaindered
Meanwhile!

TO DISCOMBOBULATE
Kimutai Kemboi Allan

I switch between different personalities
To taste the other guys
They that make merry all day
I want them and their fun

I dance alone in my dark room
Away from the curious eyes
They know that they know me
A soul atrociously introverted.

My neighbors may hear the tapping
Rubber soles furiously attacking the floor
Strange noises across the walls
I can hear their murmurs.

I am the truant being
Rushing from one mask to the other
The smiling silent neighbor at day
A wild bat dancing furiously at night!

HOW MY BROTHER PRONOUNCES HOME
Tajudeen Muadh

the last time my brother travelled, he told me his body became a mirror where he sees fear as an aftertaste of flying.

He says, "I'm sick of all the breaths I lost in my lungs, I'm sick of water letting me drown in it. Then, I recover how he covers himself in his skin, how he wishes his home is not a burnt skin.

Now, I learn to call nostalgia as a juvenescence, a revival, a poem going back into his body, as memories and as water.

my brother pronounces home, as a poem, dilapidated from the metaphors on his tongue, how he recollects himself into his skin, learning to love his past and how he covers his body with longings for days dead.

MY HOME, IS NOT A CADAVER OF ROSES
Tajudeen Muadh

that I write about grief doesn't mean my body is a steel, I, glass. This poem opens from the footage of a CCTV capturing how a poet was kidnapped. I recite them into my nerves as stanzas dying, as verses learning the language of survival.

Sometimes, I ask if God has a voice, because a poet is God's way of creating beauty.

a newspaper headline carries the obituary of a boy burrowed with a body bulleted, I wonder if it means my home is a hymn, a symphony. I firefly, I rose, I call this home a baby learning how to crawl from death into breath, how the mothers in this home are poems learning to write off worries that hung in them.

I know my home is not a cadaver of roses, because one day, a poet kidnapped will be freed, and God's voice heard, a bulleted boy will learn to whole the holes in his body and a mother will one day learn the languages of joy and this home is/will be a garden I learn to tender just as I tender the grief in this poem.

BREAKING
Tajudeen Muadh

they say you need to break into years of dust before you crawl back into yourself, I burgeon my body into wraps of refrains.

They say a poem is how we look at the sky and pluck stars, I carry myself into fireflies morphing themselves into oxygen, water and everything lucid.

I find no peace and all my wars are done.
I fear and hope, I burn, I freeze. - A poet

I break into wits and into days I run into things clinging to the past, a bildungsroman, a poem, a canvas painting my body into itself, an ode to nostalgia, and a poem resuscitating into a butterfly.

Pieces of Mirrored Light
Isaac Kilibwa

Do not despise
The gathering of fragments of light
In the person where past and future meet.
Blood calls to blood, heart goes to heart
And sometimes we live hand to mouth but,

When a man sat on the plaza
Playing from a poetry book says
The cost of an 'I love you' if you're buying
Should be an 'I love you too,'
We remember we've been loved first
Before the foundations of the world were set.

Then we grow up
And music now is intimate
Like prayer,
Like undressing before yourself.

'Blest be the tie that binds our hearts...'
Again, blest be this tent of badger skins
And hands that with oil and perfume tend
To dusty feet and wounds
Soiled in the world's rebuke.

Sandra
Isaac Kilibwa

Yester night I thought to write about you
Deep in the sky of your womb.
Chalk verses washed in the birth water of my people, tell the ancestors at last I yield.
& I wondered whether the tortoise, indifferent totem would
Fight the open emptiness kicking at giving night:

After we argue you let me plant seedlings along your spine
I nourish with the wet of my breath, flower by bloom
With petals the colour of your mother's eyes.
Soap stones jut out of your fractures and curves, fold onto waves of curling breezes.
More than this I tremble with ache to whistle a sgraffito of Korean symbols
Along your collar bone, thumb promises of forever on your red nipples, the crests of stick trees,
I'm lost in goose pimples and n-evergreen stick forests that germinate on your shins.

But I drown in flailing terror and watch you fly, gentle crane, really, I conjure you in the night
And tears circle my head running past my ears and into my hair,
My love, which is your bleeding, which is a temporary cushion
Against my place of comfort, leaks into crevices of broken clay shell

& the tortoise it sighs at how much I've scratched at the sky you've gouged around me
And wonders at the stars peeping through a gibberish of hieroglyphs
And I think I love you then, dead on my back under a horizon of snow, my tortoise,
Under your heavy head-stone for you've made a bed I sleep in.

Hope Awake
Isaac Kilibwa

It is love language to caress consciences
with haptic deaf-speak,
to argue about stars that bloom onto palms
and skulk barefoot into dreams and morning prayers
then to gesture towards a kaleidoscope of purple butterflies
etched in a ceremony of lichens.

Trauma has become purple dejavu to walk into every time that plays
the same song then falling starts. For thirty years it's learnt to expect
the undo-ing
like bereft cassette reel hoping
to spool back home, float on kind gale,
then from sin angst bleeds like time
slipping through fingers and onto the beach.
The undoing.

Keen with water as ripe abscess throbbing in labour
In a sky, palms blossom, purple heals and turns into
a dress of scars twilight's shade
when in the eyes of daughters as before so behind seen and held inside
a pulse of purple sunset.
Your beauty, the promise of happiness,
gentle gale
fleet through stills of eternity
content in promises of resurrection, where
bereft
the skin mourns
why the rain has been too long coming may it sprout as petrichor.

When a man is not a place of innocence, only sincerity and sobriety and
creeping tainted
flowers spilt into the consciousness of handkerchiefs and soaking them
in guilt,

come mine, mime words of rapprochement, come be friends once again.

Requiem: Lekki Tollgate
Prosper Ifeanyi

where laughter resounds as well as tears.
Lekki, where you were told to sing until your voices became bullets.
on that big estate, there is no rain. it is the sweat of my brow
that waters the bodies: on that big estate, there is ripe coffee & that
cherry-redness is drops of my blood turned sap.

the painting of unschooled urchins who play with
balls of rags on the noonday under the toll bridge comes to life.
molues screeching atop coal tars; iron benders crooning for steel wares.
umbrellas popping open, & apprentices carting away stray
aeolian tyres from the favelas of Ajah & Ikate-Elegushi.
nearby, I hear a shower of bells chiming with my ablutions.
Lekki: a goad that weighs; a whip that plays—

an eyesore is seeing a modern day portcullis
that cannot be brought down. roadway paved with bones
& the distant resurgence of Jakande, amid the camps of death
flowered with cotton, placards, & wooden kiosk covers.

i see a man searching for a new colour in the scaffolding
of the city; women with lynx gait, breast hard as wild orange, searching
for the remains of their beloved—

only the moon filtering through the endless palm trees can
recall the madness of our passion. we remember the day our
streets seethed with crowds like crawling millipedes.

today, our liberty still weighs upon us.
seaweed and coral brothers who have never ceased to
watch over our dead. i hear the hawking even in the pattering.
under Lekki's toll gate, vast estuary of death where all daily dreams
converge on kerbs. with my sevenfold inquisitorial eye,

more obscene than the urban wind, i have raised up through

its ripping folds.

Lekki, you are like a white seagull on the ocean crest
bright town under the white sun, flight of green palm trees,
but we have seen you grow black, since the bitter twentieth of October
when the blood of combatants for liberty was spilled in your streets.
in your bright streets, Lekki, where lights were turned off.

everyone, both stranger and hangman have drowned Lekki in blood,
its space reechoes furrowed messages heavy as a bobbin of lead
stored up insects and light and the sun's warmth.

With a line paraphrased from Wale Ayinla

Summarised Women
Prosper Ifeanyi

Where I come from, women have their mouths tucked under their skin. For them, life is a tortuous journey, and every stop, a new departure. I know of women whose feet are bloody lakes. Women who wish their husbands choked on seaweeds and hemlocks. Their roots growing at the end of an imagined sky. My grandmother teaches me a summary of her life. She says: you lose so many things in that lonely shrubbery. One day, you are a little girl holding a water pot over a tiny-throated vase. The next, you are landed in such a place where everything is strange. Where you must start all over. You feel like a child who has only just begun to talk. Or sometimes you are like an old woman, like this, finding a voice you know you once had. You cannot be a woman and call everything beautiful, because beauty is yanked before your own very eyes. I have lived from loss to loss, and just when I thought I had found my footing, the lilacs in the thorny field had become briars. In that short time, so much is lost in servitude to your husband. You promise to stop talking about suffering because sufferings are never equal. For a woman, the only thing ever picked was a choice of exile—even that couldn't happen in peace. So one day, you will sit on a wooden crane and this will be the only lesson parting your lips to your daughters. That they will know of a wilting rose dying away, and untuck their mouths from their skins.

a poem// in which freedom means my father & his inadequacies
Prosper Ifeanyi

the hollow auditorium of my chest
                swoons with echoes of a heartbeat

in my body, i am careless tourist
              held in strong arms of loose wrists   i try to explain
depression

to my mother, but it is   a party she doesn't want to be at.

i am afraid of living. i am afraid of leaving.
        the fireflies in my palm   escape without me. my mouth
can only

count reasons to stay awake—
        i like to think i learnt it when my father left

& that I will never truly know where I have been.
                                my ears & legs have eroded

i see the broken telephone sitting before
                                the narrowing of
light.

t-shirt reads: fuck shame! paper toiletries
half-full of dust & still collecting

                          i watched my heart develop an
amnesia
by which i mean it forgets
        itself over & over again—

a fickle framework. a clock i cannot & refuse to tell.

                        a dress handed down to me by my father. everything
trudged

to supplication. how a jacket becomes more reliable
than a father happens overnight—

                              but a tale of freedom is a long walk
from home.

I WHINED MY WAIST ROUND THE WORLD, A WHILE AGO.
Onatola Abiodun

I.
The World is at peace with self.
The day no longer tell days to closed eyes for night seeing
And clocks no longer sing that sonorous songs it sang while we was young.
- Colourful quests
and black no longer signals to red
like mutant in Mumdial meet
to speak truth to whosoever cares
and the shortened black hand
confusing still
- I sent my next door neighbor son to check what time it is
and he responded, 'seven quarters to nine'.
I let myself away from wilful corrections as I swim gingerly away from 'Daradele River', the very stream that birth our heads as we returned with grandfather from his farm to feed,
What an eon years I still remember how we connected through boats, rivers around hometown - Ikenne.
And today again, looking out of my windows into the World, I still found the World peaceful still
- A Russian missiles fired into Ukraine killed Sixteen.
Bless be God for blessing my misty eyes with this 'sweet sorrow'
And indeed I can testify
- we are happier than our forefathers...

SILTING 6.
Onatola Abiodun

I.
It's past 6,
the dawn should supposedly be, here. Eyes staring deep into familiar figures till all faded away visibly convincing vision and blurred again at the instance of recognition.
II.
It's after 6, this dawn shouldn't have been here.

Sun, welcoming the arrival of new night and chasing it away till it was lost, a good story in a community of no writer.

Looking through windows, darkness was the light blindfolding our eyes.

Hunters hurried home happily with their hunting bags empty of games.
III.
Looking away from outdoor to looking in, the clock still stationed self at after 6.

The riverbank refused rains, fishes too found new lover and divorcing self in prodigal of unending togetherness but on land.
IV.
The planted crops bodyguard self at harvest, daring their darling owners,

all of them joyful still as they danced home in beatings, percussions made from their empty barns. One farmer hang himself to safe as he met his rice pudding desecrated by Herder's peaceful invasion.
The news at 7, aired rather too fast.
The Anchor hurrying through editorial, learned professional in need of an unending tutoring.
V.

The government at the center in the exercise of prerogative of mercy, totally suspended the use of old currency, Our peaceful cities now in frenzy.

Citizens at the mercies of the leaders were left in the saving hands of the commercial banks for milking. A sane woman naked self-protesting across a bank teller queue when the manager said her bank balance read Zero.

We have a new emperor in town
- The POS operators, charging as their Lordship pleases. One man desirous of change set self-ablaze, inferno that kills to bring alive. Our Brothers are now the new wife at home...

/!!!\
Onatola Abiodun

I.
Do you perchance, have a shuttle in the crypt
to travel on the voyage of the spirit to God's whole own wither rand.
Of how the World, word became contradictions to the Unity, religion professed.

Here, is an harvest of Soul and I bet you let go, your religious book, contraptions
for you to be wise in this town of clarifications.

I'm sure you know
- The Crescent moon and Crosses, celestial symbolism and the traditional route to seeking God. All sacrificial.
Three trials testing but which is God's favourite?
They are all but medium through God's eyes for visibility, an inlet to His Spiritual Soul.

II.
The Pope at Cardinal said marriage to him forbidden, devoting self in whole to God whose injunction to creation was procreation and in his pursuit of holiness too, he seldom stopby at alcohol residence to check on the well-being of bottled ethanol.

Our Esteemed Man on Arabic errand is marriage closest peer, he has in his home an harem of Women and each outdoing self to prove she's the best and mostly the new wedded wife is always joyous in her sorrow.
- I think she should be aware that Our friend is every woman friend and before her he has had among them his flavoured favourite. His home a Medinah of distiller's den

And The Trado kinsmen were the most hated of the three, by the two above.
The Two who had their eyes hidden behind God's injunctions to undo the things of God at every junction.

III.
Tell me, whose handwork are padlocks hammered to trees in the deepest of the forest?

Whose venture was the fastened of different sex figurine by wools, multicolored like rainbow's rays in summer.

Whose bidding is the gulp of black powder with bottled spirit before Dawn's infant eyes to murder the day, goodnight awaiting all eyes to saint's sleeping.

I have had a fare share of all the three but in tradition I'm immersed much
- God knows, so does my paternal grandmother and my mother too.

God's madness can never be undone by His Creation sanity.
And in the profession of dance, I'm offbeat but I'm the sweet songs from the god's own ecstasy…

in this city
MK Kuol

an aged sage, long before this city became this city, once said:
a city is a noah's ark in discord. those who flee, for refuge, into it
sooner or later drown in the deluge of their own blood. then this city
became this city. & he said: *in droves, they'll flock in; people who'll stretch*
their lenses more than they'll stretch hands when discord strikes. not long ago,
a child scoured this city's corners for what to table long before he knew what
a table was as another tussled for crumbs with hounds under an
affluent's table.
yesterday, a shriveled child stretched his withered hands towards me.
a soft song sibilated a distance away: *in this city, where even the storied good*
samaritan would eschew virtue, it's to be unkind to yourself to be kind to others.
so i sidled off the scene, masked with a hollow apathy. a shard of a poem
i once wrote: *it's a normality to find a feathered fish than to find a stain*
of moral on a soul disrobed of all, sailed to the shores of my mind. back
in my [1]*rakuba,* the images of the shriveled child: *a scattered stare//chapped*
lips//a ballooned belly, rib-strapped to a flesh-bare back, slide-showed
in slow motion before shape-shifting into a monochromatic [2]*vulture &*
the little girl
in my mind. i twittered about my day. *you're no less a carter: a vulture, too.*
commented an aghast moralist before tweeting: *armaggeddon won't be when*
the falling sky crumbles onto the sinking earth. it'll be when a brother's bother
bothers not the other brother. i screamed until the silence, tending my guilt
to its blossom, drowned. the next day, i morning-chored at first crow & slid
into the streets before the night puked the sun. he stretched his hands
at me again,

---

[1] shack in colloquial Arabic

[2] An award-winning Kevin Carter's photograph taken in 1993. Carter would later commit suicide after he was criticized for "not doing enough" to save the child.

the shriveled child. i combed my pockets for a pound. *there was enough but not enough for the two of us.* the song sibilated again—this time, louder; this time, nearer.
head-bowed, i sidled off the scene—again. times like this—times when a community
will be nothing more than a mere assemblage of huts—had been prophesized.

times like this
MK Kuol

on the only newspaper stand down my street,
a bold, red, uppercased breaking news: **FOUR MEN KILLED, FIVE CHILDREN AND A WOMAN ABDUCTED IN A VILLAGE NORTH OF BOR** glares at me. i pass past unbothered. here,
where such is a normality, it takes more than breaking news
to break us down. back home, my mama strums her
wrinkled skin, humming a theme song to her grief as she's done
for the past four years since she parted with the belief grief
can be overcome. beside her, my uncle who, since he returned
from war, sits all day rehearsing the acceptance speech for his death
to his own amusement. i pass past them, too, unbothered.
inside my unlit room, i pull out my worn diary & scribble, like
i always do, in third person pronouns all the experiences i'm ashamed
to be associated with, hoping i'll overcome these ordeals one day &
use them in my motivational speeches. with little exaggerations,
of course. like *how i ploughed my garden with my teeth when i
couldn't afford tools. or how i wrote poems that convinced politicians
to keep their promises even after elections.* a friend calls. invites me
to a book reading. i pass past my papa who now says little since the war
broke out. he clears his throat, asks: *you've perfumed. where to, baba?*
to a book reading, i say. *they who want to live past times like this
must not leave their homes this late in this mad city.* i returned
to my unlit room fuming i wasted perfume. later, another friend calls, asks
if what he's seeing on facebook was true. i log in. it was. my friend & two
others had been stray-bulleted on their way to the book reading.

epitaphs
MK Kuol

the sky has emptied her bowels
        yet the gutters are still bone-dry

who could've divined the stars
        would someday outshine the sun?

isn't it suicide, too, if a man strangles
strange thoughts for the fear of being judged?

isn't it suicide, too, if a man manipulates a language,
stripping it bare to bones for the sake of convention?

my mother's blank face is a conversation i've missed
listening to. sometimes i pluck her cold smile
from the family's portrait & punctuate with it
all the poems i write about tales she'd be telling
                      my children now.

my father is not a man. he's a vowel
lunging life into the veins of a language
he doesn't even know he knows.

when i told my tutor i was worried
i might forget my first tongue, he told me:
*does one give up childbearing because
one's primigenial child has died?
improve your grades, child…*

*a man who has forgotten his language
has forgotten himself,* i screamed
until my tongue split. then quipped:
*isn't it such an irony how this society
beats us into looking for our reflections
in mirrors designed to distort them?*

yesterday, when ³nyankol in a daymare told me:
*the only way you can usher into the warm arms
of immortality nurslings of your imagination
is to ridicule them,* i laughed. & asked: *isn't it
ridiculous to think we think about immortality
here where we barely last a lifespan?*

---

[3] Nyankol Mathiang, a didactic singer often considered as the voice of her generation who passed on immediately after independence.

Bulawayo
Tembi Charles

There are two ways to describe the city of Bulawayo, the city that I love, the city of my childhood. You could say that it has very wide roads lined with Jacaranda threes whose purple leaves perfume the neighborhood. But then you could also say that Bulawayo is a city of divisions, of concrete and dust and dryness; it all depends where you are standing, and it depends on the time. All I want to say to the City of my Youth is that I long for the days when I could recognize you Bulawayo; the sound of big omnibuses, brand new and shining along Pelandaba Road, stopping at stops and picking up children walking home from Nkulumani Primary School, past teachers walking home, mothers going to the store to buy bread and milk for their husbands' tea, husbands with sore hands making their way from the city where they have been stitching shoes from hard leather, and making furniture from pine threes, many walking home, many cycling home and a few driving home to their loved ones waiting to see what they brought back from the City of Lights. When I think of you Bulawayo, I think of people who walk along your streets rushing to different places and I think of the last summer I visited you when I saw a woman sitting outside the Bulawayo Public Library suckling her baby with a box on top of which were ice mints she was selling for 10 cents each. Next to her a woman with two little boys sitting on the concrete floor holding four grass brooms she brought from her village in Gwanda. Bulawayo-I wondered why you had changed so much, why the roads had big potholes, and the grass was overgrown and the signs which said "no trespassers" still stood there rusty but strong. Bulawayo, the change that has become you does not allow me to stay, because all my memories have become desires and my desires memories.

ELES SABEM!?
Afonso Kudissadila

Sabem da Bomba lançada,
que fez a guerra findada
com mortos deixados
num país com escombros!?

Choro cantando
a música de dor
dos muitos enganados
vivendo em dor.

Onde estaria
o grande causador?
Saberia ele
dessa minha dor?

Saberia ele
do que sinto,
e que suas acções
é-me absinto.

Metralhadora comprada,
vidas coitadas
oferecidas a morte
sem salario da sorte.

Saberiam os líderes,
dos órfãos chorando,
dos sonhos matados
e dos danos causados?

Saberiam eles,
o cheiro do medo,
a corrida do aleijado
e o morto abandonado?

Conhecem eles a dor
da velha que enterra
os jovens mortos dela
vitimados pela guerra?

Sabiam eles isso!?
A dor, o medo, negro
infelizes no seu coração
chorando por sofrer má ação.

Sabem eles do âmago
causado pela solidão
de enterrar um amigo
morto de guerra, na acção!?

MARCAS DO SÉCULO XX
Afonso Kudissadila

A maior arma dos colonos
Não foi o poderio militar
Todavia,
Foi um sentimento de centopeia
Transmitida pelo veneno da política sem par
Com objectivos de criar no coração dos Africanos
 Combustões de ódios com tantas pernas.

O coração de África foi atingido
Com a munição do preconceito,
Prendida nos arames farpados da escravidão,
E todos os seus filhos,
Nasciam com a mesma maldição.

RAZÕES PARA VIVER & PARA MORRER
Armando Botelho

da vida
(re)tirei casca dos olhos
com que abraçava
noites húmidas
espirrei recolher madrugadas
quebrei caverna onde
amputavam amarelas asas
em baixa dor pintei-me
no chão paraíso
abordam dedos meus chuva
a cor rentada em gavetas
contam-me rios meus pulmões
alimento-os idade janeiro
contam-me rios meus pulmões
alimentam-me fôlego cinza

SENTI MENTALISTA(S) GLORIOSO(S)
Armando Botelho

senti largada a trazer violino
desenhei nos braços narrativa
dos desejos
é prosa a saudar meus pulmões
batuques descrevem
limite humano
ouço instante a conjugar existência
do xadrez no pretérito perfeito
quantos vulcões se endurecem
quando tem cores o vento?
quantas pedras se levantam
quando não narra mentalismo
apenas rosas na prosa?
não mais me divorcio
da gramática do tempo
tempo é mulher com
mil maços no corpo
prefiro exercitar sua voz
reinventar em cada
horizonte o instante

HOMEN
Destino Ventura

Crianças
só passam e passam
mulheres passam
de volta trazem crocodilos

o rio também passa
passa nova mente passando
almas
vazios

passa pelo tempo parado
a ver nosso rio que não passa
sagrado lugar
não canta graças às suas pedras

transpassa

quem o rio espera voltar à nascente
para trazer sereias?

FONTE
Destino Ventura

Vida é caminho que se repete
atender o último suspiro
caminho de translação alma faz
nascer no céu da boca parede é corpo

na nocturna construção
chão vida milenar nas correntezas deste corpo
cheira a flor
agridoce sabor do choro
                [muntu[4]

mulher é infinita mãe
com semente no ventre é pessoa
ressuscita descendentes

---

[4]Pessoa

nas pegadas do pássaro
Dnaffe Medina

na aberta perna do tempo
passado (f)olhar. vento.
e tu, ó Ntoyo pintado Nzadi

lungwila jinkau céu paraíso

eis que das pegadas nasce
o belo que se abre ao estigma
gigantesca formiga mu tadi ya nkixi
gigante és cá ó rico pardal

do bico teu voam cantos nsela
vestes espíritos deuses de criação !
entoam ainda hinos traduzindo paz
tais marcas assim indeléveis

dimoyo
Dnaffe Medina

MOYO,
que dedos brotassem-me paz
fosse mundo um ninho
recolhido sobre meus pés

fosse o mundo feito de cantos
era eu a canção dos tempos.
pegar terra em céu meu
negrume voo canções do vazio

eu o pássaro em mim
MOYO,
que dedos brotassem-me eterna idade

Magras silhuetas
Hélder Simbad

lado a lado
com pesados fardos nas cabeças
panos de ramos de palmeira: as duas

reconheces ó poeta: banheiras cor de milho
nas meias luas das mãos feito batuque
até serem engolidas pela serpente do horizonte
até perderem suas magras silhuetas
no temporal de poeira do Calemba-2

gira descontrolada roda da vida: engenharia à Luanda
inertes seguem acelerados caminhões
sob o nublado céu de fumo de borracha
seguem massacrando restinhos de asfaltos
ganhos dos fins riachos de água preta
plásticos papelões e comeres
da guerra civil resta
só o infindo tráfego de seres
mayombola par(a)lamentar
num vai e vem tipo feitiço chê!
– Mana Belita, boa zunga,yá!
– Mãe Cati, Deus te ouve só!

Meu Coração é sua Praça
Hélder Simbad

eu digo que vermelho é uma cor muito verde.
digo que o amor acontece precoce.
que os homens desconhecem o canto da zunga.
não traduzo encanto ,
as aves secretas engaioladas no poema
não as liberto; não derrubo árvores.
matar animais no Mayombe da linguagem
ou pô-los uns contra os outros:
advérbios degolando adjectivos,
substantivos carnívoros e verbos irregulares,
por fim, o caos, o abismo
ou o caótico circular dos objectos,
a zunga na hora da corrida.
eu digo porras. porque o verbo é automático e imita.
e a mulher se detém na cama libertando
vagipássaro húmido. Vês esse leopardo?
apenas palavra, leopardo é.
porque os dentes das palavras afiam-se secretamente.
aquela zungueira acontecia em mim como um raio.
de que cor é o sangue vermelho

o mercúrio escorrendo pelas veias
a lua de sangue o deus vermelho de que cor é
a desorientadora amarela estrela guia
eu digo que a amo que
o meu coração é sua praça os bairros da capital
e o poema se enche de orquídeas.

Bolo em Fatias
Hélder Simbad

na líquida estrada violeta termina o olhar
nem americanos nem lusitanos
navios pesqueiros asiáticos e russos

redefinição da rota da conferência de Berlim
sob o cúmplice olhar de Jack Chan e Maiakovisc
arrastão: um cardume de intenções na rede do verso

toma esta faca: disse
vês este bolo? Perguntou
é um país. ponto final.
sobre o resto todos falam na zunga

**Delírios no pulmão da noite
(Alias ou aluas?)**
Henriques Fortuna

Veio à socapa, com toda fauna nos lábios,
o riso de palanca atracado na face
disposta a pastar no parque em mim:
— dizem que tens poderes especiais.
Sim, dizem que os tenho.
— como fazes?
Bem! Não sei.
— também já não importa como fazes,
convém não importar, convém exportar.
Por que me endagas?
— ora, vim até ti porque assaltou-me o desespero.
Que há contigo?
— é que o meu mundo ficou sem fôlego,
deixei-me levar, a certa altura,
 pela sedução dos manjares espirituais e transcendentais que...
Quê?
— até agora, não sei por quais corremões me guiar.
Não entendo.
— é que deixei o pulmão em Marte
o coração em Júpiter e a mente na Lua.
Sou lunática de pedra, de mármore a transbordar.
Prova.
— gostaria que me viesses, de queijo e faca e eu de pão e cereja, faremos estrada no atalho onde se perdem deuses, ou então com o teu apito afinado pões-me na boca o som do carnaval. Depois, cada foz a atravessar o chão do lume, inunda a noite (de)lírios no pulmão cheio de nós. Ou, ainda, descemos até ao rio onde naufragam heróis, banhamo-nos de lua, botamos remos, velejamos aluados como quem busca rumo em meio ao tempo sem leme, porque te espero ansiosa no espaço sideral de mim.

Lunática comiseração
Henriques Fortuna

Dizem que as palmeiras têm voz
quem põe voz salgada na sopa do choro
mal cura a dor do rio
que trespassa a alma embargada
como faz a fauna ao dar flores
entre brocados e escombros dormentes
em subsolos de paz e gritos por pão.

Nada vem ao teu encontro
quando as raízes das lages no teu ombro
põem dó nas notas do teu choro abominado
e gora que as mãos vão com vento
que tal deixar-me ficar no tempo
à beira das tuas lágrimas caudalosas
e amparar a alma nos teus olhos?!

Que tal deixar-me florescer
atrás das sobrancelhas, ficar disfarçado
camuflar-me entre as paredes que te aprisionam
e outorgar-te sorrisos frondosos?!
Que tal as rosas, que tal os lírios,
que tal a luz entretida
na manhã da tuas dores encubadas
que tal os sonhos que ficaram em litígios?!

Rugas no Sol
Isabel Sango

Sofreu com a vida
afogou-se n'amargura
achou que tudo sabia
 peito revestiu com armadura

Tempo passeou
Juventude se esgotou
O prazer adormeceu

Derme virou manchete
Rugas no sol estampados
Tinha sapatos interessados
á todos rejeitava

Mão na cabeça, seu eu soubesse a visita
O que sobrou dela?
Nem ela sabia...

Uigense
Isabel Sango

Sou de lá..
Da terra abatida e vermelha
Do capim sofrido
Onde o bago vermelho
no leite é corrompido

De lá, onde houve matanças
Irmãos de terra, inimigos-políticos
Prometendo mudanças
Deixando cravos paralíticos

Maquelense de raiz
Do caule disperso em Mavaio
Entre o Kuilo e o kibokolo
Alquimia do amor, no interior dos ascendentes.

Vim do kikongo
Etu mu Yetu
Mono Nzeye Nvova kikongo

Sou fruto Bangu
Sou Áfrika, Afrikana
Respiro a independência
de nacionalidade, N'gola.

Intensa Paixão
Isabel Sango

Doce fraqueza
Atraída pelo andar da lua
Vento cantarolava
Na mudez da noite

Frio tenebroso
Lençóis mastigados
Azul Rosa
Estrelando filme de delírios

Solidão esfaqueada
Palavras soltas
Água descendo das pedras
Terramoto sobre 4 patas

Tempo perdeu-se
De minutos em segundos
a Consumação.

A cada minuto
João Horácio Alexandrino

Tem gente que
Se sente perdido,
Que não se entende,
E que não sente-se vivo.

A cada minuto
Tem gente tornando-se
Vítima do mundo,

A cada minuto
Tem gente que
Não sabe o significado
De amar, e faz do amor
Seu passa tempo

A cada minuto tem
Gente que vive em tristeza,
Tão triste é a vida,
Tão triste é as pessoas
Que vivem nela

A cada minuto
Me vejo dando voltas,
Dou tantas voltas,
Tantas voltas dou,
Mas não sei por onde
Vou.

Sou uma criança perdida
João Horácio Alexandrino

Sou uma criança que chora
Alegremente sem parar,
Que chora por não ter
Ninguém a sua volta,
Sou uma criança
Que chora sem pai sem mãe,

 Sou uma
Criança que vive debaixo de um viaduto,
Sinto que tanto sinto a proeza do vento
Em todo meu corpo,
Deito-me ao chão, vejo faróis dos carros
Iluminando-me como o brilho das
Estrelas sinto todo cheiro do alcatrão grudado
Em meu nariz cheio de ciliado,

Sou uma criança perdida no mundo,
Talvez nunca achada no mundo, estou
Esquecido há tanto tempo, há tanto tempo
Que não sei, que não sei por onde ir, vivo sem
Paixão, quando levanto os meus olhos para que
Possa ver o mundo sinto que não há compaixão
Neste mundo, sinto medo de pedir ajuda,
As pessoas que passam, o tempo inteiro
São mais tristes que eu,
Sou está criança que mora na escuridão,
Que vive temendo a luz, eu sou essa criança
Que não sabe, o deve fazer com a vida,
Eu sou essa criança que vive aprendendo na
Escola da vida e não nessas escolas privadas
 E públicas,

Sou essa criança que acorda sem propósito,
Vive nos confortos dos sonhos,

Que sonha em ser tudo, mas que sabe
Que não dá para ser tudo e não ter
Tudo, tudo é um grande vazio e tudo não existe

Sou essa criança que escreve este poema,
Que escreve esta brutalidade de vida,
Que chora por tanto viver que grita por
Tanto silêncio, que morre de tanta solidão,
Sou essa criança que vive em mim e que
Vive no mundo.

Muro que há por detrás do mundo
João Horácio Alexandrino

Tentei saltar os muros que há no mundo,
Que sempre me avistei em cada parede
De minha alma, paredes feita a mãos e de barros
 E água do rio,

Simplesmente nunca cheguei a saltar,
Os muros que há no mundo, pois, a solidão
Derruba um pedaço da alma, vivo sem alma,

Só um pobre que anda por aí, confesso com
Toda pureza que não sei quem sou, só sei que ando
Por aí, talvez procurando um milagre para
Fazendo de mim, corajoso, forte nas horas
De tribulação,

 É tão triste quando alguém
Perde sua vida tentando
Fazer seus sonhos tornando em realidade,
Por isso, estou aqui, andando e imaginando
E tentando perceber a vida de todos
Os modos.

guardiã da vida
Khilson Khalunga

5:30
corpo é cova
sepultando passos. voz
e canções. neste peito caminho dàlgodão

8 às 12
grito azul-de-fogo-sepultura
que se ergue nos pés. derivados
verbos do medo que se abri em mim
semântica do silêncio é caminho da morte.
— há em mim cova que me cobre o corpo

18:30
desfaço-me: corpo gaveta. guarda fogo
guarda corrida. guarda pão
que fecha barrigas às pressas da noite

plano eleito oral
Khilson Khalunga

```
        h                       v
     á                        e
           v         z
              e
        s            z
     h                    e
  á                          s
```

as eleições enchem-nos a barriga

ESQUIZOFRÊNICO TEMPO II
Luís Kapemba

Há um tilintar no altar das pragas
constantemente ressonando
cardumes de dívidas mal pagas
&
Neste altar o sortilégio d'um cordeiro negro
destilando fel nos sacrifícios dos obreiros
&
Manicômios cabendo nos dedos clérigos
psiquiatrias desenhando pegadas santas
fedendo a estercos de incompletos versos!

DUAS PALMAS DE PURGATÓRIO
Luís Kapemba

Se saio o verde dos meus braços
abraço azuis capins de asfaltos
                    há braços!

quarenta dias de mar e mo(r)to
em duas palmas de purgatório.
nas ave(i)s,
Marias em sonoplastia
e santuários à berlinda

Se acendo
o verde dos meus braços
abraço azuis capins e asfaltos
quarenta sois de mar e mo(r)to
em duas palmas de purgatório
                    Rhumm!

BICHINHOS NA PRAIA
Maria Manuel Menezes

Besouros serram a madeira em arcos,
zunem barulhentos, pequenos, poderosos.
No jango abrem galerias e marcos,
a rainha aguarda, não tolera ociosos...

Pujante alardear de pássaro vaidoso!
Réplica longínqua noutro timbre qualquer...
Será chamamento de pardal caprichoso?
Flamejante namorico de um bem -me- quer?

Porcinos aclimatados a mangas
deambulam na fauna da baixa-mar.
Procuram espertos, as bivalves mabangas,
como a natureza os fez adaptar!

Brancas gaivotas se bamboleiam
bicando no baixio víveres distraídos.
Ao sol poente, nos voos se volteiam,
em coro afinado seus sons unidos.

Pequenos morcegos, temíveis noctívagos!
na fama se apressam para nos endoidecer.
Rasantes voos invisuais e vagos,
guinchos estranhos a corresponder.
Besouro, pardal, porco, gaivota, morcego!
Feiosos, simpáticos ou não!
Procuram sombra, talvez um chamego ...
Na natureza longe de confusão.

ZUNGUEIRAS "NO" MUSSULO
Maria Manuel Menezes

Andam duas, três ou quatro, com ar jocoso,
passo ligeiro pela areia do mar.
As cores balançam no gingar airoso,
tagarelas oferecem preço a cativar.

Agitam o rolo de roupa colorido:
Panos, túnicas, saias, calças…
Um arco-íris ao vento corrido!
- Amiga, olha os vestidos sem alças!

Com a conversa do preço falada,
levo uma peça pela vaidade ou pelo coração.
Delas foi na zunga a jornada,
cedo saíram para ganhar o pão!

Com firmeza e esperança na postura,
para revigorar … uma água na esteira.
Trouxas na cabeça na faina que é dura,
é mulher corajosa esta mulher zungueira!

Menos pesadas e antes da visita da lua,
apressam os passos sacudindo as cores.
Chegam cansadas do mar e da rua,
em casa aguardam-nas os seus amores.

NÃO AO RACISMO
Maria Manuel Menezes

- "Seu"…
- Seu quê?
O primeiro cisco, depois um golpe.
Na mente um belisco, ecos e contragolpe.
- Seu...?
Tanta ignorância da humana lama!
Cicatriz cerebral de ferida na alma!
Venham falas vivas em cada boca,
informe-se qualquer cabeça oca!
Um som de trovão venha e *ionize* - Ligue o mundo!
- "Os cabelos de enrolados fios, dos filhos na casa do rei Sol,
são queratina dos átomos de enxofre, permissão do pai Sol".
Um vírus falante venha e escolarize o mundo!
- "A pele escura dos trópicos ou das elevadas altitudes, é escurecida por pigmento não branco,
fazendo frente a raios ultravioletas causadores de cancro ".
Um nevão surja, e lave infecta mente!
- "Tem beleza, sabedoria e ciência, o ser diferente! "
É preciso usar amor e racionalidade,
saber aceitar e não ser indiferente.
Recusar a vida com racismo,
lutar sim pelo humanismo.

VAZIO
Mwene XI

Infinitos silêncios
Pazes, tréguas
Pactos imbuídos
De desapegos
Não quero novos começos
Esse é o meu fim
O vazio é tudo para mim
É de lá que vim
É aconchegante,
Despreocupante
Perfeito para alma errante
Espírito galopante
Faz do Prado seu harém
Um jogo que convém
É impotente a existência
Sem rédeas
Então o vazio convém.

ÁFRICA ERRANTE
Mwene XI

Espinho pelo caminho
Machuca os pés
Um passo de cada vez
E alcanço a sensatez
Não estou sozinho
Tenho-vos comigo
Oh, espíritos do além

Ancestralidade triunfante
Em prol da África querida,
Ferida,
Dividida, desfolhada.
Concebida
Dá luz a uma geração sem norte
Outro ora forte
Hoje abandonada a sua sorte
Devorada por abutres
Que prometeram suporte
Essa é a África errante
Caminhando ao abate

MENTE
Mwene XI

Ausente do presente
Oh mente!
Que tal desfrutares do agora?
Olha o dia lindo lá fora
A fauna da cidade e a flora
Curta a savana
Solta o espírito animal
O banheiro é uma sauna
A chuva a fonte termal
Faz mais sentido
O futuro hipotético?
Ou reviver o passado enterrado?
Es transcendente,
Desafias o tecido espaço-tempo?
Viver o passado,
Presente e futuro ao mesmo tempo
É um furo do roteiro, tiro no próprio pé
Ore mar contra a maré

NÃO JAMAIS
Ntony Kunsevi

Não Jamais
saberei dizer
do teu peito cacheado
dos teus lábios flamejantes
dos teus olhos esverdeados
irmã gémea da felicidade
congregadora de
gémeas de gazelas desavindas
silhueta de curvas perigosas

Não Jamais
saberei dizer
ao desfiar a tua nudez
ao vestir-te da brisa leve da prima vera

Um adorno de pétalas solares
Um jardim nos confins da alvorada
Um raiar de amor
Ao serpentear a brisa

Não jamais
saberei dizer
dos intangíveis lábios teus
da audácia na fragrância
do aroma da elegância
dos teus beijos soltos em prefácio de amor

MISTÉRIO
Ntony Kunsevi

Nojenta e infortunada
andas de pernas bambas
odeio-te de todas as formas

Silhueta diabólica com todos os contornos
armada em mais bela das mulheres
beleza inebriante, cheiro de ilusão
és delírio sem fim
símbolo da perdição

Como ousas infernizar a paixão
oasiana sem consolo nem fonte de agua
mal amada e desdita
obra prima de diabo

Tenebrosa tentadora
exaltas a tua beleza

Amiga venenosa da serpente
mil e uma irrealizações
ornamentas sobre o barro de desespero

Sua bunda que abundas
ungida de lágrimas douradas
afugenta almas
não minto
gemes no canto de paraíso
armada em musa, sua medusa.

QUARENTONA
Ntony Kunsevi

Ginga com vaidade
neste vaivém da tua idade
move como nzinga
a tua silhueta ondular
invoca com a tua voz
a sabedoria do mpovi

Quarentona
com expressão de menina
longas ancas esculpidas
trilogia estética
em uníssono peitoral
portadora de lábios milagrosos
seiva refinada de prazer brotar

Dia amante bruto
esculpido corpo
pelagem
tecida de algodão solar

Moldagem de deusa
afeição facial
um adorno luminoso
fogo vivo
ar dente
cristal
lina deusa de fogo
fogo dos artifícios
voluptuosos

Tetas erectos
na horizontal corpo

Esbelta estrela

de mimos celestiais

AR TE FILOSOFANDO
Satchonga Tchiwale

Não precisa, o poema ser político
a fome dizer ao poeta, basta!
os versos por si só comentam
para tal, se o político faz poemas
o poeta canta a liberdade
o país vive contente

RUPTURA AOS PATRIOTAS
Satchonga Tchiwale

Nascem ideologias, a pedra
ou quão bom é o político
que se despe das injúrias
que do povo emana satisfação
ao nascer como pessoa
nascem os sonhadores
(…) uma vez ideo-legistas
um autentico filósofo.

RUPTURA AOS GOVERNANTES
Satchonga Tchiwale

Quando se vive do povo, a progressão
em meio pleito oral, a mente um livro se torna
desce a progressão, governo, povo, voto
ironia do sábio, com diplomas se torna deus
sábio que é, mais uma vez opressor, o inverso
voto, povo, governo, até os deuses festejarem

LABIRINTO
Simão Nzombo Antônio

Se fez questão esperar
tão sombrio a razão que partiu
incógnitas na lentidão
e a pressa que não alcança!
procuramo-nos na história da mesma geografia
movidos para o hall da festa
um co(r)po cruzando o itinerário
um conhecido desconhecido no se não
e
Louco movo-se a alcateia entre rebanhos
na fanfarra surdida
onde ki-zomba à surdina
não me desfiz da caravana
quem me encontrar, me acha

SERENATA ANORGÁSMICA
Simão Nzombo Antônio

Esculpir sobre a língua o falo
tecer a fala-anciã de karma
ao desnudar a mu(Lemba)
esculpir os poetas de poesia taciturna
a prosa é um pano quente
que queima á quente frias memorias
esculpir os poetas imberbes
a bacia revirando a cidade
o beberão na volúpia
e todas putas tristes
não há orgasmos
sem preliminares

Lweji
Vítor Ricardo

Belisco a macula da criação
Detalhe por detalhe
Alternando a cadência
Ora predador, ora presa

Arrefeço o calor diário
Nas trincheiras do seu Atlântico
Entre os relevos da sua formosura
Elevo-me a um ser superior

Deixo os ponteiros do meu relógio brincar
O seu tic tac ecoar
Com o mais macio dos pinceis, pinto as suas loucuras
Ela, musa
Eu, Picasso ou Picatchu!

O seu olhar criptografado
Um abajur mitológico
Traz infernos, soluços, canções
A medida que sigo dedilhando cada fragmento seu

Mulemba solitária
Vítor Ricardo

Sinto saudade dos passeios
Do grito da noite
Dos embriagados
Que já cantaram aqui, as suas maiores decepções

Só ficou um vento teimoso e solitário
Que vive a minha volta
A tentar entender a dúvida que a vida deixou

A mulemba solitária que aqui ficou
Tem medo do tempo e dorme amargurada
Sem ninguém para lhe aquecer nas noites de cacimbo

Vento, venta-me devagar
Velha que sou
Solitária que sou
Temo não poder ver, outros amores a viver aqui
Os seus melhores dias

Grotte secrète
Laroche Ngodjo Abata

Mane bola, au cœur de la foret
Éclairé par la blancheur du jour
Guidé par le murmure des ancêtres
Bercé par le chant de la nature
Je glisse vers l'essence de la vie

Sur les feuilles des herbes
Se dispersent sur la rosée
Les rayons du jour
Éclairés par ces bulles lumineuses
Mes pas se couchent sur le sentier
En direction de la grotte secrète
Maison de la sagesse ancestrale

Élèves...
Laroche Ngodjo Abata

Sur l'asphalte
La semelle de la chaussure tambourine
Sur l'asphalte
Les pas se succèdent
Les traces du brouillard s'estompent
Laissant place au jour

Le sac au dos
La tête pleine de rêves
Les élèves courent à la source
La source, pour se couvrir d'intelligence
Pour s'armer contre tout danger

Sur leurs routes s'étalent les épines
Sur leurs routes le danger se dessine
Sous leurs pieds s'effondrent
Tous leurs rêves, tous leurs mondes d'idées
Engloutis par la barbarie des hommes

Souvenir
Laroche Ngodjo Abata

Dans ma mémoire
Se dessinent des souvenirs
Souvenir de nos temps passés
L'ombre de ta silhouette
Fait la ronde de mes pensées

Sur les premières marches de l'aube
Ta voix fait écho dans le vent
Pour caresser les souvenirs
Enfouis dans ma mémoire
Pour faire danser sous mes paupières
Nos cœurs joyeux d'antan

Aujourd'hui la pâleur du jour
Ride mon visage
Le froid matinal gèle mon cœur frêle
Seul la beauté du crépuscule
Le sourire de la verdure
Maintiennent ma flamme en éveille

Village des fous
Arnold Mondo K

Ainsi tout tourne en rond,
Ainsi tout bascule bas-haut
Sans aucun doute,
Sans aucun remord
Mais en vain.
Si mon mal m'était pale,
Tous crieront balle.
Alors ce dieu d'absurdes
Les incitent dans la bande
Sans arrêt et sans trêve.
Sa liberté volée au volant
Et sa raison fermée au barreau,
Quand mon bien me rime.
Dans le bain de la palabre,
Les vautours me tournent en rond
Et m'invitent à la cour.
De là les vers de ma défense riment
Aussi bien que leurs verres de terre.
Si leurs yeux chantaient le blanc,
Mais leur poésie serait poétique.
Hélas ! leurs rythmes ne riment pas
A ce que rimassaient les mots.
A leur vue, le noir est pur,
L'honnêteté à leurs oreilles
Est un crime et le malhonnête
Se conjugue comme une valeur.
Le voilà en folie mon toit.

A la belle aux cieux
Arnold Mondo K

J'aime quand elle chante,
D'une voix charmante,
Au son mélancolique
Suivant un doux rythme
Qui jaillit la gaieté
Et dorlotant l'été.
Sa tendre chanson,
Enveloppée d'un pétillant son
Chasse le tourment,
Par une atmosphère du vent
Soufflant humidité et froidure.
Voilà la belle aux cieux,
Qu'on appelle pluie.

Cantique africain
Arnold Mondo K

Dans le fond du noir,
Se réunit un culte du soir,
Suivant une culture amère,
Amenant les gens à la mer,
Avec l'envie d'essor,
Et dans l'ironie du sort.
Au bout de chaque cirque,
Défile un perroquet,
Sous le brouhaha grotesque,
Tantôt au rythme philippique,
Avec augure et joyeux augure
Mais qui ne laissant peu d'espoir…

Bronzitude
Michel Dongmo Evina

Notre écorce naquit des abymes colorés
Moulée dans l'argile soyeuse du Zambèze
Elle était faite de la même souche que l'iroko
Et sa légende remonta les latitudes enchantées

Bronzés par trois millénaires de mépris
Nous n'avons pourtant cessé de marcher
En rangs fourmillants
En rangs arc-en-ciel
Insensibles aux lots de crachats brûlants

Les injures coulèrent en flots
Ruisselant sur ce roc d'épiderme
Et nous avons quand-même marché
Couvant sous la rudesse de cette échine
Une somme d'humanité incandescente

Oui, nous sommes foncés depuis l'aube des temps
Sous cette croûte cramée git notre mère Soleil
Et nous venons dire ces vérités inquiétantes
Aussi drues que le grain de notre écorce capillaire
L'humanité naquit dans une couche de mélanine
Votre haine s'écroulera au seuil de notre pigment.

Le feu du milieu
Michel Dongmo Evina

Appel au secours dans l'arène des étreintes
Quand ton corps brûlant pétille d'impatience
Ta peau effusive diffuse des étincelles
Je plonge mon corps la langue la première
Dans le cratère de tes coulées d'orgasme
Et je m'embrase tout entier dans la fournaise de la fente
Et je m'étale patiemment sous les combles de l'amour

J'étouffe de plaisir dans la couche ardente
Où ton souffle chaleureux m'édicte la cadence
Je m'abandonne et je me perds
Je te touche et je me trouve
J'éprouve la morsure de ton sein insoumis
Je sens la brûlure de ta fente en furie
J'éructe des râles sourds je cogne je trépigne
Je te laisse m'emporter ô feu
Dans les torrents du milieu en furie.

Réminiscences
Faustin Junior Embolo Embolo

Les rires agonisaient dans l'enfer
Celui des citadelles écartelées
Où l'espoir vivant mourait dans les révoltes des profondes fortunes infidèles
Des hommes aux chants étranges d'orgueil aux milieux des lieux sataniques
Des mains infécondes
Sales et imprudentes
Je n'oublie pas dans ma mémoire sauvage
L'humiliation des générations de l'indigénat
La guerre pour une guerre sans enjeux
Mais dans un jeu de sang et de blessure
Les yeux cherchant la plénitude dans l'irrésistible amour
Sont toujours affamés dans les meurtrissures indignes des travailleurs forcés
Des existences humiliées
Jusqu'aux tragédies des perles dévalorisées
L'Afrique devient le martyr
D'horribles démons
Je n'oublierai jamais le désastre salué par les voisines
Herbes sauvages vulnérables et impuissantes
Parfois mulâtres
Parfois métisses
Parfois négresses
Nous sommes le nombril du monde
Une ceinture qui se rompt dans l'écartèlement d'une terre meurtrie
Nous sommes le tonnerre au sein d'une île inexistante
Nous sommes la source de vie
Où est attaché le cordon sombre des sources profondes de sueur
Nous sommes les peuples faibles tristes et doux attachés aux ancêtres
Et sur le bois de la mort les syllabes de la flamme crépitent
Et leur résonnance laisse jeter l'odeur de nos poils brûlés
La misère des hommes transfigurés
Des soirs aux violentes fessées

Non je n'y pense plus
C'est tragique
C'est fou
Mais c'est vrai
Le temps n'entache pas ce souvenir
Il est couvert d'une bâche protectrice
Que rien ne peut ternir
Souvenir de violence chanson de misère
Antienne de barbarie
Je suis le prisonnier de mes cauchemars

L'Afrique contaminée
Corneille Mbonyi

Je suis une étoile, fils du Royaume Kongo,
Derrière l'Afrique, j'ai ressenti les fouets de Tipo Tipo,
Bêtement, la blanche planète a tissé le calvaire sur nos terres,
Sans pitié ni âme, le sang a coulé, c'était l'enfer.

Refrain :
Je suis une étoile, fils du Royaume Kongo,
Le calvaire sur nos terres, le sang coulant en longs flots.
Je suis une étoile, dans l'obscurité, je me noie,
Mais je brille toujours, malgré le poids de l'histoire.

Je suis un Soldat qui a vu l'aurore zaïroise percer,
Après une nuit sombre, qui a versé des larmes sur l'Afrique blessée,
Comme on dit que l'abeille ne vise que le visage du miel,
C'est ainsi que les blancs ont persisté dans leur bêtise,
Sans lâcher d'un centimètre la carte du Congo,
Et Lumumba, cette cicatrice immortelle,
A été emporté par des complots,
Faute de frapper à la porte de la Paix et de la justice

Refrain :
Je suis une étoile, fils du Royaume Kongo,
Le calvaire sur nos terres, le sang coulant en longs flots.
Je suis une étoile, dans l'obscurité, je me noie,
Mais je brille toujours, malgré le poids de l'histoire.

Je suis le témoin de l'Europe qui a contaminé l'Afrique,
Nos esprits drogués subissent des effets tristes,
Et c'est ainsi que l'éléphanteau veut couper les cornes de l'éléphant,
C'est ainsi que le Rwanda nous chasse de notre terre.

Refrain :
Je suis une étoile, fils du Royaume Kongo,
Le calvaire sur nos terres, le sang coulant en longs flots.

Je suis une étoile, dans l'obscurité je me noie,
Mais je brille toujours, malgré le poids de l'histoire.

A toi Afrique
Serge Billo Ebanga

Mon cœur battait dans tes mains fleuries
Où j'ai cueilli des bouquets de soleil exquis
Pour combler le vide de mes insuffisances endolories
Ô Afrique berceau de la vie !
En rode chant je te dédie
Mon hymne à la lisière de la poésie ;
Toi ! royaume des vertes prairies
Vers qui accourent mes désirs.
Soir et matin je te bénis !
Sois préservée de l'oublie ;
Mieux des tragédies
De tes enfants désunis.
Mon cœur bat encore dans tes mains
Où mon âme t'exalte terre de ma patrie.
Ô Afrique terre de mon sang, de toute ma vie
Je porterais tes ailes vers le lointain infini.

J'ai rêvé de toi Afrique
Serge Billo Ebanga

J'ai rêvé de toi Afrique !
Belle et prospère,
Sans grillage ni frontières.
J'ai rêvé de toi Afrique !
Libre et indépendante,
Sans entrave ni contrainte.
J'ai rêvé de toi Afrique !
Unie et pacifiée
Sans conflits ni inimitiés.
J'ai rêvé de toi Afrique !
Forte et respectée,
Sans corruption ni inégalités.
J'ai rêvé de toi Afrique !
Et je rêve toujours,
Peut-être qu'un jour
Ô Afrique seras-tu Afrique ?
Celle de mes rêves,
De tous tes enfants le même rêve.
Ô Afrique mon Afrique !

Oublier
Chandra Feupessi

Il n'oubliera jamais ce jour
Où vos deux cœurs entrelacés
Encore dans les feux de l'amour
Se sont séparés

Il n'oubliera jamais ces interminables heures Où au bord de la mort
Il ne lui restait plus que les pleurs
Pour ton réconfort

Il n'oubliera jamais ce regard
Plein de tristesse
Parlant dans le noir
Pour avouer tes faiblesses

Il n'oubliera jamais tes dernières paroles
Dites entre tes derniers cris Qui eurent pour rôle
D'affaiblir son cœur déjà meurtri

Il n'oubliera jamais cette fille Qui gisait là
Avec qui il voulut fonder une famille
Avec qui il rêvait autrefois

Best New African Poets Collaborations
Curated by Tendai Rinos Mwanaka

Mwanaka: *These are the suggested areas we will collaborate around, I. Bewitching and witchcraft, II. AI writing impact on future African creativity, III. Erotic poem, and IV. Towards a multipolar world, Russia and NATO War in Ukraine and growing influence of China*

I

Blessing Chingunda:

Witchcraft, magic and miracles are all sleight of hand tricks.
Nothing of great importance.
Unless we're delusional, superstitious maybe we can say witchcraft is real.
But as of now there's no amount of evidence to substantiate it.
Aliester Crawley the father of witchcraft promulgated openly that it's all a sham.
Nothing of significance with it.

Joseph Hope:

May God not allow witches and wizards to have anyone's time.

There are surely many things we can't explain that are real.

We can have false evidence. We can have no evidence.
Some knowledge is just beyond humans.

Muhammad Sulaiman:

I am an ardent pan of lie
As I preach only the blue
I was even called a sinner
Within the world of liars.

If you could recall my pitch
Yesterday it was in climax
But today turned anticlimax
As I lost foot sure to speak.

You may Not need to cry
Since today it is Monday
No! It maybe a Sunday
But tragedy has been in its peak.

Here the Sahara is blazing
And the sky seems to flame
Greenery dried like aridity
While it's amidst of August.

Do Not tell me he's deafer
While he danced in our songs
And even pay for its melody
But today he acts like a baby.

Abdullah Khalid:

In shadows deep where secrets dwell,
A realm of magic, cast its spell.
With whispered words and gestures rare,
Witchcraft weaves its mystic air.

From herbs and potions, spells take flight,
In the cauldron's simmering light.
Moon's phases guide their ancient way,
Through night and dawn, where spirits play.

A dance of elements, earth and fire,
Witchcraft's craft, never to tire.
The witches gather 'neath the moon,
Their power rising, like a tune.

Enchantments woven, old and new,
In whispered incantations true.
With wisdom passed through ages past,
Witchcraft's lore forever cast.

So honor well the witches' creed,
In witchcraft's power, find what you need.
Respect the craft that's lived for ages,
Witchcraft's history, in its pages.

William Mpina:

The power of witchcraft
Pulses in the beat of drums
Unseen but heard

Abdullah Khalid:

"The power of witchcraft
Pulses in the beat of drums
Unseen but heard."

A dance of magic, secret and divine.
Unseen but heard, its whispers rise,
Across the winds, where enchantment lies.

Adesola Oladoja:

"The power of witchcraft
Pulses in the beat of drums
Unseen but heard."

"A dance of magic, secret and divine.
Unseen but heard, its whispers rise,
Across the winds, where enchantment lies."

They see you through enchanted prisms

hear the hollowness of your heart's beat
wait, till hubris pronounce you supple meat

George Chisimdi:

Jealousy and greediness
   Laziness and procrastination
    Selfishness and foolishness
      Leads to witchcraft
       If it exists, if it real
    But our fathers believes it
It is real and courses havocs
They fly in darkness to their pray
Spiritually attacks physically seen
 They are human, they are evil
    Always care, evil at dark.

 What of our prophets and priests
  Says when the lord haven't
 Given peace, trouble escalate
Who collects from the wretched
 That has turn homes in to turmoil
    Even our corrupt leaders
 Witchcraft, witchcraft, witchcraft.

Okey Ifeachor:

Their gathering is in the coven of evil
To milk the fountain of buoyancy dry
And disconcert peace and joy
Why kill the joy you created not?

Beautiful smiles of innocence on the face
Laced in heart full of vice and odium
To browbeat the unwary
Heaping monumental afflictions

The staccato noise in the night
Herald their ominous arrival
To unjustly thwart destiny
Witches and wizards, guests no one wants to have.

Night is their day for harm
When mortals peacefully sleep
When dawn comes, they feign guiltless
Rejoicing for the pains they caused

Mzinyathi Jabulani. B:

Then witchcraft became a race thing
Conveniently forgot their word: witchcraft
The craft of witches
The wizardry tucked away
Shakespeare perhaps had seen it
"When shall we three meet again
In thunder, lightning or in rain?" he end rhymed
Could it have been the figment of a fertile imagination?
They even talk of goblins
The secretive dark arts are not exclusive to one race or are they
They did not use owls
For they saw wisdom in the owl
Perhaps they did not ride on hyenas
Flew on eerie nights on brooms
We flew on winnowing fans

Mhondera Chenjerai:

Go and tell your mother,
That i said she's mother bitch!
Oh sorry, mother witch!
But what if witch and bitch
are one and the same thing?
For both are night-riders
And killers!

The only difference existing
between them, being
that a bitch kills slowly, kindly and sweetly
from a poisoned passion
and piece in her abdomen,
but a witch kills fast, rough,
and painfully so,
from her poisoned thoughts

Bolaji Tola:

Should I join you to stone the witch,
When she is my mother:
That towering owl
That you claim ate the baby.
Of course she screeched yesterday,
The Newborn is dead today,
No need to guess who the culprit is...
My mother,
Your witch.
For before time you claim she flies,
Legs on the wall,
A summon from the coven,
That woman you want to stone,
Is my mother.
To you she's a witch,
For me she's the switch.

Abdullah Khalid:

She is a switch, a match to darkness
Killing slowly but firmly in breeziness
A predator covered with sadness
A beacon of inhumane madness!

John Attah Ojonugwa:

My mother tells me to shout the name 'Jesus' whenever an owl hoots at night.
My friend, Ifeanyi said an owl fell in their compound and transformed into an old woman.
I didn't see it myself but my mother tells me they can do a lot of things.
'Are they more powerful than God?' I ask my Ma.
'No. But you must be wary,' she said.

I've been told they fly with the brooms and some with the leaves from certain trees.

I guess they strike fear in the hearts of mortals when they attack or do the things they say they do.

But how much do you know about your next-door neighbour?
Do they smile but think differently?

What if you're the witch you bind and cast in church?

Mwanaka:

And then maybe the owl is just being an owl, and you are the witch?

John Attah Ojonugwa:

What we believe in matters here. Some believe an owl is an ominous sign. Europeans may see it just as a bird but not most of Africa.

Okey Ifeachor:

Mother is right
The agents of the witch...
Owl, gecko, and bird
Come with the wind of fear
To monitor its victim and drain strength of boldness

Tell the witchcraft operators: I am not a victim

For the blood of Jesus Christ covers
Making me a victor as I dwell in the secret place of my Creator.

Mwanaka:
What we don't know doesn't exist until we know it... We can't be here and there

Mhondera Chenjerai:

My mother, being a hard worker -
Always say, if you want to be a witch or wizard,
Just be lazy,
And once lazy you become jealousy,
And once jealousy, you kill…
She would say by wishing others bad in life

Okey Ifeachor:

But am I a witch?
Do I begrudge another's success?
Do I covert my neighbour's resources?
If I shoot down my brother with my tongue
Tell me why I should not be tagged a witch.

Abdullah Khalid:

Wishing others bad in life, her choice
Manifesting envy in her voice
Nomatter the preaching, she can't rejoice!

Okolo Chinua:

This begins with fingers and a collection of hands...
Mother says to open your eyes here is to walk backwards to everything you've ever believed...
Owl feet falls and the rain draws 'flections...
Lightning screams and Mother's eyes are several faces dancing...

The water rises...
When the wind explodes I am still...
An arm darkened... a moon appears...

Emmanuel Tumwesige:

Standing at crossroads wondering
Like a fly that has lost a scent
The magic of the world unknown
By the mind of the living flesh.
The wind with arms roaming through
Untamed but evoked to do the unthinkable;
A swam of bees chased mlefu out of his hut
Mlefu had gone undercover for flying at night
Aiming at silencing the spirit of his brother
The one whose death was told by the hooting owl
And he is out by the art of the dark hand.
Dark or powerful? I am at the crossroads.
My sister's seventh still birth proves the talk
Her husband belongs not to her but a co wife
Is it magic taking the new borns?

II

Mzinyathi J. B:

What fuel do they run out of
It cannot be jet A1
For the winnowing fan
Stories galore of the sun rising
Revealing the dark arts or sciences
Nothing but their birthday suits
The jeering ensues
Acres of media space taken
Later it is all the din of silence
And the cycle continues

Abdullah Khalid:

In depths of silicon minds, lights flicker bright,
Intelligence synthesized, within AI's sight.
An era dawns, where knowledge shall rise,
Artificial brilliance, boundless skies.

William Mpina:

AI's uncensored thoughts are like smoke,
That drift towards a starving soul.
The mirror exposes no angels,
But regrets for its blunders.
It cannot be me but itself,
With its uncircumcised errors.

Mzinyathi J. B:

Will these glorious days be gone
Of sitting and raking the minds
Angling for those words
To attempt capturing feelings
To pour forth those emotions
Are we kissing spontaneity goodbye

Bolaji Tola:

Now he can read my mind,
That tiny wizard of AI,
Is it not the small town,
That nearly destroyed Josh people,
That city that claim mastery over my thoughts.
They say she can speak my heart,
And gather my thoughts of yester years.
It can smell my butt and describe my shit.
It can summarize my thoughts
In few inglorious words…

Should I be scared?

Mhondera Chenjerai:

Does it make a difference
To say artificial intelligence
is cramming?
Once upon a time, time upon once,
and upon once a time,
They call someone a genius,
For repeating jb channon, and the madness that
'a' is a small letter of 'A'
'b' is small letter of 'B'
'd' a small letter of 'D'
'q' a small letter of 'Q'
'e' a small letter of 'E'
'f' a small letter of "F'
'g' a small letter of 'G'
'h' a small letter of 'H'
and so on, and so on,
even when all such doesn't make sense,
that if a letter is Z, why when it changes size,
should it also change form,
when the aspect and effect of capital letter, and small letters,
only applies to an increase and decrease of the letters,
but without dismantling, disintegrating, disfiguring the letter
to form another letter completely different from its former capital or small?
Like if the letter C is c, X is x, Y is y, V is v, J is j, K is k, P is p,
they still remain that letter in complexion, collection,
compilation and completion,
regardless of age, weathering them,
from their youthful stage to their senior of age.
I am a fool because i am opposed
To the mind of this supposed genius,
Where they bully every reasoning, astute - divergent, contrary
Simply because it doesn't fall in what they

Categorically identified as upheld philosophy and intelligence

Okey Ifeachor:

I will not be afraid of that being without soul
I will not be afraid of the bloodless entity
That says what I input into it
I'm still the master of the entity that knows not the joy of relationship
AI is still subject to my dictates
I'm at the top, I am the greatest.

Okolo Chinua:

AI
Like a sceptre at the edge of a knife to leave this walk to you is to dedicate a circle to an arc...

For every train you hold the proper rails appear and the circle grows day by day, a razor-toothed slide...

In every water is a hammerhead crest and to swim the rivers of this craft is not to have fins...
To swim here is not to see a needle straight-lined...
It's to appear one-eyed, bled and dusty...
To be drowned, welcoming each bubble with sinking bliss...

Everyday a circle larger, razor-toothed and flowy...
But not in this water that welcomes and takes...

Bungada Pedro Fernandes:

Sem leis
Entre doutrinas mecânicas
Culturas inquebráveis
Normas dos homens
Leis ditas naturais
Vou amar-te

Sem leis
Sem regras
Vou beijar-te
Sem ética
Sem virtude
Vou abraçar-te
Sem aspas
Sem vírgulas

O que sinto por ti
Está além de preceitos
Serei turista em todas as zonas do teus peitos
Tomarei as águas da tua nascente
Banharei com as águas dos teus céus
O meu amor por ti
Está além de dilemas
Sem pacto social
Sem acordo divinal

Treparei as tuas montanhas
Quentes e salientas
Aliciantes e suculentas
Não temerei o céu
E não me esconderei dos olhos
Da fauna e nem da flora
Tampouco das águas ou das estrelas

E se o sol fechar os olhos
Farei da noite uma amiga
Da lua uma vela
Sem vergonha dos ouvidos
Do vento e das paredes
Gemerei prazer e alegria
Paixão e satisfação
Sem medo de algum juízo
Enfrentarei qualquer sentença
Porque o que sinto por ti

Está além de qualquer natureza.

III

William Mpina:

Milky fluid flows in a soft pipe
Like sugarcane oozing its sweetness inside me
The taste is sweet and sticky
Like honey on my tongue

I close my eyes, and savour the flavour
Drums beat in my ears like a gentle breeze
My legs open with warmth
I feel like I am flying in a state of pure bliss

The drums stop beating, and I open my eyes
The milky fluid is in me
The taste, the feeling all nice
This moment of pure joy is mine to keep.

Bungada Pedro Fernandes:

A retórica do amor I
Por que esperar a aprovação do Nada
Por que aguardar a aceitação de pós
É popular que a velhice é inevitável
Cheia de fraquezas e inutilidades
Enquanto temos o corpo erecto
Que tal aproveitarmos o momento
Vamos navegar nas marés de um ao outro
Tu tens o tesouro
E eu a chave
Que tal abrirmo-la
E repartimos os prazeres da caixa

Por que te refutas do que queres

Encobertas-te com vestes de pombos
Mas os teus olhos esbanjam as nudezes dos teus desejos
Por que te prostras diante de ovelhas
Não vez que o teu coração ♥ ♥ murmura?
Levanta-te daí e venha comigo
Vou mostrar-te outros templos
Que não castigam os olhos
E nem os joelhos
Conhecerás os pontos da felicidade
Felicidade em F
E em G
Os teus heroicos e limitados lábios
Implorarão por beijos
Que despertam qualquer nascente

Por que te prendes nas cortinas dos teu aposento
Não és tu o titular da tua própria vida?
Por que queres ficar na plateia tediosa do teu recinto
Não vez que é limitada tua vista?
Venha experimentar o sol
Abraçar o ar
Pisar o solo
Dançar sub os sons da natureza
Venha ver a lua e as estrelas
Sentir a humidade da terra
Ouvir as conversas das aves
E descobrir as sensações que o teu corpo esconde

Mhondera Chenjerai:

Myself won't write a piece on erotic!
For what needs to be known
About penetration into someone's abdominal wound?
Is it the screams like streams?
Someone obsessed in such ecstasy,
The diver having dived into a pool of delight?

Why should I write about it anyway?
For penetration is penetration,
Whether one leg up, one leg down,
At 45°, 60°, right angle, or @ 150° bisected 75° at diagonal:
the karataker, trying it differently at 180°.

Why should i write,
What even my esteemed editor
And curator of sanity deemed never subject for discussion!
Why should i write, what my father intimated to me?
as a do in private and say in it public;
for the gods of morals never to hear you
and curse you,
for telling in open
what you do in private?

Otieno Kennix Odera:

She now lies there beautifully dressed in nothing,
I see moisture in her eyes,
The dark dot;
Fights the heavenly whiteness,
I stare at her lips,
The lower one is sensually curved,
I look again,
Her toned lower back;
Gives me a slow burn,
Hitting me like fire,
Activating a sweety air of desire in my torso,
I groan internally,
Edging closer,
She gladly accepts my affection,
Eliciting more fire,
I slip my tongue on hers,
I can now feel her hot flesh,
She gasps softly in pleasure,
I plant more gentle kisses;

On her already burning skin,
The nipples; are attentive,
I am already hard and weak,
She pushes her body tighter against mine,
I see a woman in need,
She lifts her head to show the desire burning in her eyes,
I kneel between her,
Her entrance is ready,
We've risen to the peak of pleasuredom,
I lie low,
She passionately grabs my lower back,
And guides me down between her,
Her inner limbs;
Are soft,
The wetness is already waiting for me,
I slowly wheel my jellied steel inside her,
Then with more haste,
Oh! No!
Am dripping,
I grab her low with all my might,
Biting my teeth,
Praising the maker,
Telling HIM am "coming" right now,
She has now strangled my abdomen,
Am dying,
From sugar,
Nobody can rescue me; not even her,
Don't save me,

Joseph Sikali:

You have eyes that gaze through my heart
Your voice sparks irresistible natural fires in me
I know you are someone's but your body is a drug
It gives me amnesia I forget I am someone's too
In my depression you are the therapist I run to
Every session in closed doors intertwines our souls

I eat every fruit in the basket on your office table
From the delicious pawpaws to the sliced apple
Days with you, I breathe life to our slow deaths
Heaven knows you're my favorite sin regardless
I can't let you go even when it's right to do so
So keep me as a secret for a little more nights
I will hold on too while satisfying your needs
Don't go hungry on me, eat the forbidden fruit

Mzinyathi J. B:

Woman, close the windows
Keep out peeping toms
Double check the door lock
The unique dance is on
No audience allowed in here
Let Eros and Cupid croon
After the gyration fall into exhaustion

Woman, let me drink
Drink alone from your well
That I may try quench my thirst
Let me alone enjoy your cooking
Though I still remain insatiable
I will always yearn for more

Okolo Chinua:

The night gleams of you...
And your smile is a moon's bow.
Your skin a vanilla sip that I soak in,
You speak, the words come out golden...

With every spiral I immerse in this valley of flowers,
And there is no promised bliss better…
The archs are a treasure sought,
and the sounds a desire relished..

The sun drowns in you,
At dawn you emerge, full of light...

Bolaji Tola:

I knew that path so well,
Along the two soft ridges.
I've kissed that ocean:
Your deep red sea.
Walked the narrow path,
Along the dark forest,
I know my way,
Even in darkness.
Know how you ring,
My wifi detects your hotspot.
Seen you vibrate
An effort not to ring.
Know your password,
Enter at will.
Recently,
In the day,
I lost my hay,
A new password,
Beneficiaries?
Not me.

Emmanuel Tumwesige:

So sweet is the sound of the running water of the river
As it kisses the rocks with the splashing
Bringing a sensation deep in my veins
Like an oar rowing a bride's boat after the vows.
Pulsing as it swims deep to the wellhead
Then returning with sweetness of the moistness
From within the river.
The thudding of the oar within calling a melody
In moans of undivided attention synchronous

With the sound of the river.

Okey Ifeachor:

The spasms of joy
After the trusts that generate soothing moans
Moans that leave memories of insatiable hunger for another round of meal like Oliver Twist asking for more.

Come for warm embrace that turns seconds into day
Launching the duo into realm that forgets the pain and hurt...
Memories of peace and joy

The duo knit into one as two head leech
 The rain claps on the roof in a night of amorous bliss
Thank you for the unity of souls.

IV

Okey Ifeachor:

It was tough battle of the round leather
Balance of power almost at equilibrium
Then, the shot of good success came
The goal of victory
Spontaneity of the moment...
Race to warm embrace as staccato noise of bliss filled the air
Kiss of victory planted in global glare
Without thought of indecency
As hot blood of patriotism flowed in the veins

The nerves are cool
Interpretations...
Bring the kisser to slab of death
As the kissed trumps non-consent
To assuage gender activists

But in the spur of the moment
Enjoyed the kiss of triumph

Dance the dance of victory
Let not the kiss of victory leave
sour taste in the mouth that sang for joy
Celebrate the feat seldom achieved
Let the joy killers not triumph
Let Luis Rubiales savour the joy of victory.

Mzinyathi J. B:

Wield a big stick
Thrash the barking dog
When the owner steps forward
Give him a hiding too
The owner bawling
The dog whimpering

The lessons must be learnt
Zelensky see the bodies
Your cities lie in ruins
You thought it was a walk
A leisurely stroll in the park
That was a declaration of war
Courting your brother's foes

This is not devil worship
Innocent lives are lost
That is collateral damage
Your handlers know better.

In Libya they had their way
In Iraq they killed him
Just like a mangy dog
The war criminals go free
The hypocrisy of the ICC

That is in plain sight.

Your American ally stood by
Our people butchered in Mzansi
Many more massacred in Zimbabwe
Not a finger lifted against apartheid
Not one lifted against racist Rhodesia.

Putin we stand by you
Put the bullies in their place
We will never forget our friends
Those that were in the trenches with us.
That assault rifle the symbol of our liberation
Yes, the Russian made AK47.
Giving them sleepless nights.

Stop those war mongers
Stop those NATO demons
Wake up and smell the coffee

Okey Ifeachor:

Tell me not who to associate with
We are in a world full of choices
I'm not tied to your apron string
Your enemies must not be my foes

Are you not on the same table
Drinking tea as equal chums?
Where then is your enmity
That you abhor my relationship?

My freedom should not be subjugated
To your perceived superiority
What you thought was a run-over
Is lingering beyond your imagination

Though you destroy my inheritance
And kill the innocents
Though you multiply widows, widowers and orphans
My resolve stands firm as the rock of Gibraltar
Kowtowing not to your selfish whims

The world is a global village
Village of peace and love, not of hate and war
Let me be the way I want to be
Force me not to drink from your cup of intimidation

Best New African Poets Interview
Tendai Rinos Mwanaka

This year I decided to give poets I have worked with in the BNAP series an opportunity to interview me. Here are their questions and my responses

Mzinyathi Jabulani B: How many hours a day do you sleep, if you ever do? My question is drawn from the fact that you are a multidisciplinary artist- poetry, photography, music, painting, prose- the list is endless.

Tendai
I sleep the normal hours most of the times, 6-8 hours a day…but 4/5 hours are fine with me some days. Sometimes you are enmeshed into what you are doing you lose track of time, by the time you check your clock, its 2 am. I usually stop working at that time…but some days I stop with night's fall, watch movies on Netflix to around10, sometimes binge watch movies upto 2 am. I don't force myself to write let's say short stories when I don't feel like it. I create what I feel like creating since I work across several fields I can always find something I really feel like doing. At other times I fill in the uninspired hours doing routine work like publishing, promotion and sometimes editorial.

Jabulani: When did you start recording songs? I realise now that some of your songs are getting airplay?

Tendai
I started recording music in 2022, when I worked with South African gospel musician Sefako Mamabolo to record my first album, Logbook Written by a Drifter. In the process I attuned myself to the process of recording and producing music. Thus my next album, Architecture of Loss, I recorded it myself, so also the latest album, To Seed and Grow Stronger. But music has always been in me from when I was a little boy. I was in the school choir in grade 2, all the way after school, at church too. But I started making music by doing the dj mixing route around 2010 but that didn't please me. I felt like an interloper. So I decided to learn to play instruments, in which I started with mbira

nyunganyunga in 2014...ever since I have been composing to mbira, I added marimba, keyboard, hosho, claps, drums etc

Jabulani: You continue to publish poetry even if it is not very profitable. What motivates you to carry on?

Tendai: Joanne Kyger said, "poetry is about continuing poetry." We make poetry for the love of making poetry. That's why we are still making poetry.

Jabulani: It seems that your songs are getting airplay abroad and not in Zimbabwe. Correct me if I am wrong? Why is that so?

Tendai

I think with that attitude I have of making art because you want to make art...the kind of art you want to make, not what someone else wants me to make...you have to do the same with publicity and promotion. You have to find the channel that wants to publicise your kind of art. I tried local radios, I think they are mostly interested in popular music...not the music I create, Art music. So I had to try to find radios out there who might be interested in my kind of music, that's why my music is being played abroad

Oscar Gwiriri: Bnaps are anthologies of poems authored by poets from different countries. How did you manage to reach out to poets in such many countries when you started the project?

Tendai

I think it was a novel idea for African poets at that time. There was no regular, open, continent-wide anthology of African poetry that was being published anywhere in Africa or abroad, so poets were excited about this new avenue and responded well. We also publicized the call for submission as widely as we could, even in some newspapers like The Zimbabwean. I was also connected with African poets through journaling my work in African anthologies especially those in South Africa, so these poets could easily trust and identify with what I was attempting to do, as they already knew me.

Gwiriri: Bnaps is a series of anthologies. What's your vision?

Tendai
We are going to keep it open for many more years to come. And I also want to expand it into an international festival whereby we will host the poets for a reading, performances etc...I have always wanted to start that in our 10th year of publishing, so I hope next year we will start this journey

Abdullah Khalid: How do you think your diverse talents influence the way you perceive the world around you? Do you find that you have a unique perspective due to your varied artistic background?

Tendai
I think I had the varied perspective already and loved to explore different fields (by the way I am a trained marketing professional, worked in the marketing fields for 4 years before I quit it for poetry again) and multitask, and its art that's benefiting from it. I grew up in a family that allowed free spirit. My parents, even though they didn't like it, supported me as I went through the processes of becoming the artist I am today.

Khalid: What advice would you give to aspiring artists who are interested in pursuing multiple creative passions? How can they effectively nurture and develop their skills across different disciplines?

Tendai
Just flow like a river... you will figure your way the river does

Andrea B Matambo: What systems do you use to generate INCOME from your artworks and writings?

Tendai
I do a lot of online advertising of my work. Keeping the content flowing on my pages. I also push my work into all sorts of Medias so that it might be reviewed. I also work with a good distribution

company, African Books Collective, who help me getting my books into international spaces I couldn't access from Zimbabwe

Mzinyathi Jabulani B: Do you have any formal training in photography and painting?

Tendai
No I don't have any formal training in the arts. I am self-trained, and this is how I have always wanted to go about it

Jabulani: For Zimbolicious Anthologies and BNAP Anthologies you have co-edited most of these with many poets, writers, editors what is the motivation behind this approach?

Tendai
I learned this from the publishers I worked with, you can only be generous as an artist. The publishers I worked with gave me the opportunity to learn the trades, so I need to give the same chances to others, allowing them to grow…

Abdullah Khalid: How did you first discover your passion for poetry, writing, music, and painting? Were there any particular experiences that inspired you?

Tendai
Each came in its own time. As I noted previously, I started music in grade 2. I was a good actor in dramas growing up. We were also exposed to all sorts of visual art, especially sculpture. I remember we had what was called Art Corner in the classrooms where our sculptures were displayed. We grew up doing sculpture, ceramics, and all sorts of crafts. So art has always been there. Writing or poetry came later, as a blessing in disguise. Whilst I passed every other subject I sat for in O level, English got the better of me. So in trying to revise and rewrite it, I was drawn into reading novels and literature books, this is what I carried with me out of high school, the love of reading. And thus I also started writing, thinking I am figuring how to improve my English,

only to realize a few years later I was infact writing something publishable.

Khalid: How do you manage your time and energy to maintain proficiency in multiple artistic disciplines? Are there any strategies you use to balance your creative endeavors?

Tendai
No, I don't balance my creativity, as I noted above I let it flow. I don't mind creating let's say more poetry than essays. I practice balance in other areas of art business like editing, mentoring, publishing, promotion etc…

Khalid: How do you approach collaborating with others, both within and outside your artistic fields? Do you find that your multidisciplinary skills enhance your collaborative abilities?

Tendai
Yes it does…all these skills help me when I collaborate. I know as an editor what I am looking for from artists. I know the process of editing a book, so I try to give artist space to figure their way about an activity.

Abdullah Khalid: As someone who excels in various forms of expression, how do you envision the future of your creative journey? Are there any new mediums or projects you're excited to explore? How do you handle moments of creative block or burnout? Are there specific strategies you employ to reignite your inspiration when it wanes?

Tendai
I never get blocked. As I noted I only create what I want to create…thus if I am not feeling like doing painting, I leave it alone and do, instead, music…that might inspire me to go back to painting with a fresher mind. Yes there are always new areas I am interested in exploring. I am also an avid gardener and farmer so it's something I also do. I think I would also love to travel, take pics and write about

new places and spaces. And in the future I see myself gravitating toward filmmaking too.

Khalid: Are there artists or creators who have significantly influenced your work in all four areas? How have they impacted your artistic style and approach?

Tendai

I have loved the Americans a lot and been exposed to all sorts of writing and art coming from the US. I love Eastern European, Jewish and Japanese writers

Emmanuel Tumwesige: There are a lot of pieces of art that describe the African culture, in your work you endeavor to portray the African spirit more so through the instruments you use. Do you think we have said a lot about Africa but the listeners are just deaf? Do you think there are other ways the 'African message' should be brought to light so as to lift the initiative?

Tendai

I think whatever we will create is always African, because that's our home, it's our outlook. We can never tire of trying to create. Our market is smaller and thus it's hard to make a living out of it. We feel the listeners are deaf...but I think it's just poverty, most don't afford the artworks. It has discouraged other artists to pursue art. But we can only continue making art- *poetry continuing making poetry*

Otieno Kennix Odera:

1. What's your worst experience with poetry?
I can't figure any...I have loved the journey

2. What would you be doing if you were not Artist?
Farming, and I am doing that already. I love the feel of the soil sifting between your finger, wet, darkly, earthy and how our fingers can create food and beauty through the soil. So it's continuing poetry, maybe. That's the same love I have with cooking

3. How has your ART changed the world?
I can only talk about how it has changed me. It has grounded me, made me like myself…I hope that's how it has affected others too

4. Why would you wish everybody was a poet? If at all you do?
I don't wish it, I think everyone is a poet…we have different ways to express poetry.

Thank you

Mmap New African Poets Series

If you have enjoyed *Best New African Poets 2023 Anthology*, consider these other fine books in the **Mmap New African Poets Series** from *Mwanaka Media and Publishing:*

I Threw a Star in a Wine Glass by Fethi Sassi
Best New African Poets 2017 Anthology by Tendai R Mwanaka and Daniel Da Purificacao
Logbook Written by a Drifter by Tendai Rinos Mwanaka
Mad Bob Republic: Bloodlines, Bile and a Crying Child by Tendai Rinos Mwanaka
Zimbolicious Poetry Vol 1 by Tendai R Mwanaka and Edward Dzonze
Zimbolicious Poetry Vol 2 by Tendai R Mwanaka and Edward Dzonze
Zimbolicious: An Anthology of Zimbabwean Literature and Arts, Vol 3 by Tendai Mwanaka
Under The Steel Yoke by Jabulani Mzinyathi
Fly in a Beehive by Thato Tshukudu
Bounding for Light by Richard Mbuthia
Sentiments by Jackson Matimba
Best New African Poets 2018 Anthology by Tendai R Mwanaka and Nsah Mala
Words That Matter by Gerry Sikazwe
The Ungendered by Delia Watterson
Ghetto Symphony by Mandla Mavolwane
Sky for a Foreign Bird by Fethi Sassi
A Portrait of Defiance by Tendai Rinos Mwanaka
Zimbolicious: An Anthology of Zimbabwean Literature and Arts, Vol 4 by Tendai Mwanaka and Jabulani Mzinyathi
When Escape Becomes the only Lover by Tendai R Mwanaka
ويَسْ مَرُ اللَيْلُ فِىَى ثِفَنَـتي...وَلِـعْمَام by Fethi Sassi
A Letter to the President by Mbizo Chirasha
This is not a poem by Richard Inya
Pressed flowers by John Eppel
Righteous Indignation by Jabulani Mzinyathi:
Blooming Cactus by Mikateko Mbambo
Rhythm of Life by Olivia Ngozi Osouha

Travellers Gather Dust and Lust by Gabriel Awuah Mainoo
Chitungwiza Mushamukuru: An Anthology from Zimbabwe's Biggest Ghetto Town by Tendai Rinos Mwanaka
Zimbolicious: An Anthology of Zimbabwean Literature and Arts, Vol 5 by Tendai Mwanaka
Because Sadness is Beautiful? by Tanaka Chidora
Of Fresh Bloom and Smoke by Abigail George
Shades of Black by Edward Dzonze
Best New African Poets 2020 Anthology by Tendai Rinos Mwanaka, Lorna Telma Zita and Balddine Moussa
This Body is an Empty Vessel by Beaton Galafa
Between Places by Tendai Rinos Mwanaka
Best New African Poets 2021 Anthology by Tendai Rinos Mwanaka, Lorna Telma Zita and Balddine Moussa
Zimbolicious: An Anthology of Zimbabwean Literature and Arts, Vol 6 by Tendai Mwanaka and Chenjerai Mhondera
A Matter of Inclusion by Chad Norman
Keeping the Sun Secret by Mariel Awendit
ه‫تَعْ‬‫ل‬ُّ‫ب‬‫و‬‫تَ‬ ُّ‫ل‬ِ‫ج‬‫س‬ by Tendai Rinos Mwanaka
Ghetto Blues by Tendai Rinos Mwanaka
Zimbolicious: An Anthology of Zimbabwean Literature and Arts, Vol 7 by Tendai Rinos Mwanaka and Tanaka Chidora
Best New African Poets 2022 Anthology by Tendai Rinos Mwanaka and Helder Simbad
Dark Lines of History by Sithembele Isaac Xhegwana
a sky is falling by Nica Cornell
Death of a Statue by Samuel Chuma
Along the way by Jabulani Mzinyathi
Strides of Hope by Tawanda Chigavazira
Young Galaxies by Abigail George
Coming of Age by Gift Sakirai
Mother's Kitchen and Other Places by Antreka. M. Tladi
Soon to be released

https://facebook.com/MwanakaMediaAndPublishing/

www.ingramcontent.com/pod-product-compliance
Lightning Source LLC
Chambersburg PA
CBHW070308230426
43664CB00015B/2675